GOING VISUAL

USING IMAGES
to ENHANCE
PRODUCTIVITY,
DECISION MAKING,
and PROFITS

ALEXIS GERARD and BOB GOLDSTEIN

WILEY

John Wiley & Sons, Inc.

To Dany, Valerie, Nicolas, and Stephan

To Katrin

Published by John Wiley & Sons, Inc., Hoboken, New Jersey
Published simultaneously in Canada

For general information about our other products and services, please contact our Customer Care Department within the United States at 800-762-2974, outside the United States at 317-572-3993 or fax 317-572-4002.

Wiley also publishes its books in a variety of electronic formats. Some content that appears in print may not be available in electronic books. For more information about Wiley products, visit our web site at www.wiley.com.

Library of Congress Cataloging-in-Publication Data:

Gerard, Alexis, 1953–
    Going visual : using images to enhance productivity, decision making and profits / Alexis Gerard and Bob Goldstein.
        p. cm.
    Includes index.
    ISBN 0-471-71025-3 (cloth)
    1. Business communication. 2. Visual communication. I. Goldstein, Bob, 1947– II. Title.
    HF5718.G45 2005
    658.4'5—dc22
                                    2004028847

Printed in the United States of America

10 9 8 7 6 5 4 3 2 1

Contents

Acknowledgments

This book would not have been possible without the backing of the broad and diverse Community of Interest that formed around the project as it unfolded—smart, forward-thinking people from many different fields, all of whom share in the vision that the mainstream use of images is transforming interpersonal communication. Their myriad contributions in the form of information, insights, counsel, and support were invaluable.

We're grateful to the many businesspeople who took time off from their demanding schedules to open their companies to us, and tell us about their experiences *Going Visual*—their successes, the pitfalls they encountered, and their infectious enthusiasm. Our particular thanks to those whose companies are described in this book: Sally Carrocino, Bob Dickey, Dennis Dillon, Jim O'Leary, Russ Mason, and Linda Rudell-Betts.

Our thanks also to the visionary executives at the many technology companies who embraced this project and supported it with their time, influence, and resources. At Adobe Systems Bryan Lamkin, Michael Hopwood, Kyle Mashima, Steve Saylor, and Cari Gushiken; at Eastman Kodak Dan Carp, Carl Gustin, Jim Stoffel, Anthony

Sanzio, and Joe Runde; at Epson Dan Steinhardt; at Hewlett-Packard Vyomesh Joshi, John Meyer, George Lynch, Phil McKinney, Tara Bunch, Ted Wilson, and Pat Kinley; at IBM Gail Whipple, Adel Al Saleh, Dean Douglas, Peter Guglielmino, Amy Lipton, George Schlaugenhaupt, and JD Zeeman; at LightSurf Philippe Kahn, Robin Nijor, and Dave Kumec; at Microsoft Charles Mauzy, Amir Majdamehr, and Craig Munde; at Nikon Jerry Grossman; at Sprint Pierre Barbeau, Phil Garrison, Jeff Hallock, and Nancy Sherrer. Also Chris Yewdall at DDD Digital Dynamics, David Shoenfeld and Mark Knighton of NextEngine, and Bob Goligoski at Sandisk.

Similarly, our insights into the research and thinking at some of the world's leading academic institutions were a key influence on our work. Our gratitude in particular to Michael Bove and Glori-anna Davenport at the MIT Media Lab, Rudy Burger and Stefan Agamanolis at the Media Lab Europe, Mary Tripsas at Harvard University, Victor Lacour at USC's Integrated Media Systems Center, and Pieter Lechner at the UCLA Visual Communication Portal.

As first-time authors we would never have been able to find our way without the initial help and guidance of Colleen Dunn-Bates, Angela Rinaldi, and Regina Ryan, and we would never have been able to put together an appropriate book proposal were it not for our association with Jill Nagle. Our warmest thanks of all to our terrific agent Denise Marcil, and her team, Maura Kye and Mary-Kate Przybycien, and our wonderful editor at John Wiley & Sons, Debra Englander and her team, including Greg Friedman, Kim Craven, and Alexia Meyers.

So many more people have helped in so many ways that we can't list them all here, but with apologies to those we will inevitably have forgotten we wish to express our gratitude to Anthony Bannon at the George Eastman House, Scott Brownstein and Georgia McCabe at Fuji, Willis "Buzz" Hartshorn at the International Center of Photography, Gibboney Huske at Credit Suisse First Boston, Guy Kawasaki at Garage.com, the Future Image team, Joe Byrd, Tony

Henning, Paul Worthington, and Heidy Bravo; and also Gayle Cline, Jean Barda, Robert Blumberg, Steve Broback, Katrin Eisman, Mark Kalow, Dot Krause, Jacques Kaufmann, Shannon King, Pedro Meyer, John McIntosh, Evan Nisselson, Doug Rowan, Rick Smolan, Eric Poppleton, Broeck Coleman, Rob Steinberg, and Victor Raphael.

Finally, on the production side, our thanks to Mark Jaress, for graphic design, Kathy Jessee, for transcription services, Jeff Weinstock for invaluable copyediting, Ira Nowinski and Scott Highton for photography, Cindy Edelson for graphic services, and the team at North Market Street Graphics, including Christine Furry and Lainey Harding. Last, we thank the following corporations who provided equipment in support of the project: Adobe Systems for image editing and organization software; Epson for printers and media; Hewlett-Packard for laptop computers, flatbed scanners, digital cameras, and printers; Nokia for camera phones; Sandisk for removable media for digital cameras; Sprint for camera phones; and Sony Electronics for digital cameras.

Foreword

When I was first asked to write a foreword for this book, I declined because I was very busy with the tour for my own book, *The Art of the Start.* However, after I read the manuscript, I found I liked the book very much and quickly agreed to write the foreword after all. I decided that since the book evangelizes visual communication, I should "write" a visual foreword.

This is the first pictorial foreword in history—at least as far as I know. It depicts how I predict the book will affect you: It will give you tactical, actionable ideas about how to use digital photography to improve your business.

My business is venture capital, so I meet with hundreds of entrepreneurs,

listen to their pitches, and get back to them later. My problem is that it's hard for me to remember their names and to recall their whiteboard diagrams.

Guy Kawasaki
Managing Director
Garage Technology Ventures

Introduction:
Getting the Picture

This book addresses the question, "What is the best new tool I could use to significantly improve my business?" The short answer is *images*—and their power to communicate. *Going Visual* is all about putting that power to use.

We live in a world of images. Images are everywhere, in magazines and catalogs; on television, billboards, and web sites; on our kitchen refrigerators, our desks, and the walls of our offices. Humanity has been using images to communicate since painting on the walls of caves at the beginning of recorded time.

Consider that when most people embark on a personal event— attend a birthday party, start a vacation, visit a theme park—they instinctively take a still or video camera. Through images, we communicate the most important messages in our personal lives: the birth of a child, the purchase of a home, a family reunion.

Yet images remain largely unused by individuals in the one part of their lives where they spend the most time and need the most powerful tools—interpersonal business communications. Other than in the fields of advertising, insurance, and sales, the power of the old

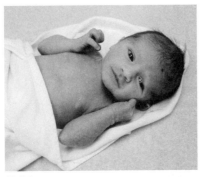

Child

Home

Family reunion

saying "A picture is worth a thousand words" has yet to be harnessed in the world of business. In the main, we still describe people, places, objects, and processes with text-heavy memos and reports rather than simply showing images of the same. Most businesspeople have yet to take advantage of the immense potential inherent in images to communicate information more completely, more efficiently, in greater detail, and with greater power of conviction than can words alone.

If you were to canvass a typical office today, except in certain image-centric professions, you would find that very few people carry a camera of any kind. While we all know that a picture is worth a thousand words, most businesspeople still laboriously type thousands of words to express an idea instead of taking and sending a picture. If an executive were contemplating renting a billboard location, would he or she not be better off considering this shot over a written description?

If a maintenance department needed to specially configure a truck to its specifications, wouldn't images like these speak far better than words ever could?

Isn't something as simple as reporting a broken piece of furniture better done with an image such as this one than through a verbal description of the problem?

Most of us in today's workforce have grown up believing that using photographs and video in our own communications is either too difficult, too expensive, or beyond our abilities. We, as a society, are just now awakening to the tremendous power to communicate visually that the past 20 years of imaging, computer, and telecommunication technologies, combined with the worldwide information network, have brought to our homes and businesses.

For the past 15 years we have consulted with many of the foremost leaders in business, technology, education, and the arts on the potential of imaging technology to fundamentally improve communication. The scientists, technologists, educators, businesspeople, and artists we have met all have a similar passion for the new power of images. We did one memorable and enlightening interview with Peter Guglielmino, chief technology officer of IBM's Digital Media Division, who put the concepts of *Going Visual* in the context of a sixteenth-century classical music concert.

"Video and images portray information above and beyond what's captured by text," Guglielmino said. "The semantics of what's happening during a conversation or a presentation are captured differently when you do it with video or images than when someone's just taking notes. Think about a Bach concert in 1500, when he was performing himself. . . . Now, 500 years later, we have access to the information of that concert, faithfully recorded as the notes of a score, but we don't have any record of the event itself. We've lost all the semantics that describe what it sounded like, what the interchange was between the different sections of the orchestra, how the audience reacted—in brief, the whole scene. This is completely applicable to events today. If you just record them textually, you're missing a tremendous amount of information."

Guglielmino's observations speak to the inherent limitations of language as a description tool. Beyond simply our own inabilities to produce detailed and accurate descriptions, the challenges are numerous. Think about the problems that can occur in the simplest of scenarios, one person communicating with another who is in a different location or time:

- Describing something accurately can often require the use of specialized vocabulary—whether through a musical instrument, a tool, a part, a plant, or an article of clothing. If either party doesn't comprehend that vocabulary, the communication can turn into miscommunication. The wrong tool, the wrong part, leading to frustration, wasted time, and wasted money.

- In a global business environment, language differences can play a huge role in creating miscommunication. In Guglielmino's example, the language was sixteenth-century German. A descriptive image cuts through language barriers and provides a form of information that needs little or no translation.

- Different people observe different things about the very same scene based on their culture, their age, their personality, and their interests. A Bach concert would be viewed in very different ways by a musician, an architect, and a clothing designer. An image allows the creator to show more detail than can be accurately described in text or speech, while giving viewers the opportunity to focus on details in the picture that suit their purposes.

- Images provide an information-rich visual record of people, places, and things at a specific moment in time. Historians viewing an image of the Bach concert would find a wealth of information from which to draw. What may seem unimportant today, and therefore may not be recorded in a written description, can turn out to be crucially important later on. Images recording the daily progress of projects can prove to be valuable assets in tracking and evaluating business processes to help resolve disputes. A visual history can be as profoundly important to a business as images are to a newspaper's archive.

When viewed from the perspective of the daily text-only communications that flow through any business, loss of information detail occurs at every retelling—the risks of erroneous, unclear communication—and the potential consequences grow exponentially. Images transcend these issues because they are a global language, with an infinite vocabulary that is familiar to everyone.

That is not to say that our enthusiasm for the use of images is at the expense of language. Far from it: We are using words to write this book. Words and images together are much more than the sum of their parts. Philippe Kahn, the visionary founder of LightSurf Technologies, told us, "If a picture is worth a thousand words, then a picture with text is worth 10,000 words." Going one step further, alluding to the musical element of the Bach concert, he said, "When you add audio to pictures and text, that's worth a million words."

As we describe in Chapter 1, what separates us from the sixteenth century is that today's technology makes it possible to use, in practical business circumstances, visual tools that capture the scope of events and the full richness of the information we wish to convey. As Jim Stoffel, chief technology officer of the Eastman Kodak Company, observed about the place of images in our modern world, "There is an exponential increase in the order of pictures in our lives that really is about the quality and character of our communications."

Having formulated the theory that using the power of images to communicate can significantly improve business processes, which we have dubbed *Going Visual,* we went looking for business cases that could illustrate its application in the real world. Did the theory truly work? Could individuals and companies use simple visual technology to significantly change and improve the way they communicate? What could stand in the way of implementation? How could ordinary businesspeople apply the concepts? How would *Going Visual* improve their businesses' productivity, decision-making process, and bottom line?

In our two years of field research, we were gratified to find numerous instances of people and companies launching *Going Visual* strategies in their everyday business lives, migrating from primarily text-based communications to image-rich methods, thereby saving countless person-hours and dollars. We found that the democratization, through low cost and ease of use, of such technologies as digital cameras, computers, camera phones, camcorders, and the Internet is empowering ordinary, nontechnical people to *Go Visual* in areas of business communication that had previously always been the province of the written or spoken word.

Here are a few examples from organizations large and small where the inefficient use of words has been replaced by information-rich images:

- A major airline equips all of its maintenance crews with digital cameras so they can visually document physical problems they encounter on the aircraft. These pictures can be instantly sent to a remote supervisor to get immediate advice on how to fix the problem; then they are stored in a database and used to help solve that problem the next time it appears.

- A landscape contractor never leaves her house without her digital camera, because she uses images to communicate to management and clients the current conditions at job sites, the progress of various projects, and suggestions she has for design elements. She uses the images to get approvals for change orders, creative decisions, and troubleshooting.

- The police force in Yakima, Washington, has equipped its entire fleet of 32 police cars with wireless video capability that is linked with global positioning systems, the radar system, and even the lights on the roof of the police car. As soon as police officers flick on their lights to begin a chase, the system automatically backs up 10 seconds and begins saving the video images from that point. With this capability, the entire event, including the moments leading up to the chase, can be recorded on searchable digital video so that police can afterward provide investigators with a visual context of the incident.

- A dentist in Florida, Dr. Paul Epstein, who specializes in aesthetic reconstructive dentistry, uses images he takes of a patient's teeth and face to study, plan, and collaborate on procedures with technicians and specialists. He creates a mold of what the reconstructed work will look like and photographs it in place, in the patient's mouth. The patient can then share the images with family and friends, who may help them make what in many cases is a life-changing decision. Epstein says that the use of images has brought his practice "to a whole new level. . . . It just makes communication so much easier. . . . It helps me become a better dentist."

- A cosmetic company's field sales reps, who service department stores, photograph product display cases, end caps, and shelves to produce a visual report on in-store contract compliance. The photos are invaluable in verifying whether the correct product was in the agreed-upon location on a given date.

We found all these stories, and others like them, so compelling that we would have liked to include all of them in this book, but that was not feasible. Selecting only a handful to examine in detail was no easy task. In the end, we picked the four that demonstrate most clearly how a *Going Visual* strategy can be applied in a business of any size. These case studies include a multitude of uses that are applicable to any type of industry.

We looked for the commonalities among these stories: How did the idea of *Going Visual* first appear in the organization? Who brought it up and why? What were the concerns that had to be overcome? How did *Going Visual* fit with the big picture—the organization's goals and values, its human elements, as well as with the specific task at hand or improvement desired? How did these businesses go about measuring the impact of *Going Visual?* The challenge, which the pioneering businesspeople who are profiled in this book have addressed and answered, is how to incorporate images into everyday communications in a natural, effective way. We looked for and studied the patterns of their success and have devised a five-step *Going Visual* methodology that summarizes the principles, practices, and processes these companies are using on an everyday basis, which is presented in Chapter 2.

The businesses profiled in the following chapters run the gamut from tiny companies to large multinationals. They have one key thing in common: Their experiences show in great detail how *Going Visual* has sharpened their competitive edges.

- Chapter 3 examines how a property management firm that was 100 percent text-based before discovering that pictures were worth thousands of words methodically went about testing, evaluating, and implementing visual communication processes with clients, suppliers, employees, and government agencies. This company's story starts with a single digital camera and ends with 50. A project supervisor observes, "I used to write a nine-page report; now I send a picture."

- In Chapter 4 we profile a self-employed sales representative who had never taken a picture for work use until she discovered the power of the digital camera to, as she puts it, "revolutionize her business."

- In Chapter 5 we speak with executives at a nationwide retail garden and home furnishings company that now uses images from camera phones and digital cameras as the very fabric of its global communications across functions as diverse as product sourcing, manufacturing, and store management. The senior vice president of merchandising declares, "Every single day I get images that represent what used to be a lot of words. . . . It's now become the way of doing business."

- In Chapter 6 we examine how a global communications services firm extended a few images used as a simple sales tool into a *Going Visual* strategy that improves every aspect of its operations. This company established a sophisticated archiving structure that allows all its branches and departments to rely on an integrated base of visual information to significantly streamline their operations. The director of digital services succinctly described the importance of *Going Visual:* "We use images everywhere."

- Chapter 7 reveals how managers in information technology, human resources, and project development at an international entertainment enterprise use videoconferencing to manage project teams dispersed around the world. The company's real-time-collaboration project manager explains that *Going Visual* "doesn't just save you money, it changes the way you do business. It accelerates business."

- In Chapter 8, we examine five new key directions that imaging technology will take in the coming three years and how they will enable the firms we profile and all others to go further visually— to further increase the efficiency and richness of their communication processes.

In most cases, the overhead, learning curves, and technology required to begin adopting a *Going Visual* strategy are all surprisingly ordinary. The trigger to action is a lightbulb moment, an "Aha!" flash, whereby a key decision maker sees how a simple shift to using images in everyday business communications can produce dramatic improvements to the bottom line. These decision makers are our guides through the various stories, and they relate, in a very down-to-earth way, how *Going Visual* has fundamentally improved their businesses. All started with tactical uses of visual communication— a specific type of image for a particular informational need. As the value of this new method became apparent, the use of images spread through the organization: marketing, sales, project management, operations, finance, facilities management, manufacturing, customer relations, product research, design, quality control, human resources, information technology (IT), maintenance, public relations, facilities management, dispute resolution, operations, procurement, planning, and, significantly, accounts receivable. All were dramatically enhanced by the systematic integration of visual communication inside and outside the company. In all cases, visual information became an indispensable component of the business. Just as you might find it hard to imagine how you ever did business before fax, e-mail, or FedEx, these companies can't imagine how they did business before *Going Visual.*

When dealing with a topic that involves technology, we recognize that businesses need to rely on rock-solid, proven products that are available *now.* For that reason, these examples we cite are founded entirely on currently existing, affordable technology. We also provide a realistic three-year perspective—a time frame chosen to match common strategic planning cycles—on technology developments that will further expand the possibilities for visual communication. Nothing you read about in this book is science fiction; these products already exist in working versions that we have personally seen, and they are on product release schedules that will make them widely available to the public.

Perhaps most gratifying to us, we were struck, time and again, by the high level of enthusiasm with which the businesspeople we interviewed spoke about their experiences in using images to communicate. They were quick not only to describe the practical benefits relating to enhanced decision making, productivity, profits, and customer relations, but also to convey their visceral excitement at being able to communicate in such a natural, detail-rich way for the first time in their lives.

We hope you see a piece of yourself and your business in the stories that follow. You are invited to visit our web site, www .GoingVisual.com, where you can post your own visual communication stories and join an online community dedicated to exploring the opportunities, challenges, and innovative solutions that are emerging in these early years of the Visual Age. We wish you success as you embark on your own *Going Visual* journey.

PRACTICAL EXERCISE

Go to your kitchen and stand in a spot that gives you the most complete view of the space. Try to describe, in a written document, everything you see from that single viewpoint: the appliances, cupboards, dishes, glassware, sink, floor, lighting, walls, knickknacks, and so on. You will quickly discover that this process could take a very long time indeed and could fill many pages of text. Now stand in the same spot and snap a picture. In a split second, all those details are captured. If you have used a digital camera, the information is instantly in a format that can be easily shared with virtually anyone so that they can see what you saw. You have a common point of reference to use in discussing the kitchen's details with an interior designer, a painter, a plumber, an electrician, a floor refinisher, or a cabinetmaker. You have just experienced that a picture is worth a thousand words.

CHAPTER 1

Visual Communication: A Short History

A t its most basic, the notion of *Going Visual* is rooted in overcoming the limits humans have faced throughout all of history when attempting to communicate what they see to another individual who is in another location.

> One way of thinking about all of life and civilization is as being about how the world registers and processes information.
>
> **—Seth Lloyd, Massachusetts Institute of Technology**

One of the characteristics that defines us as a species is that we first and foremost process the world visually. Other species rely on different senses—many on smell, some on hearing, and others still on senses we don't even have, such as radar. We are engineered to be highly sophisticated seeing machines. Our brain and eyes are so intricately connected that in some respects it's hard to say where one ends and the other begins. More than a million axons (nerve fibers) are dedicated to the optical nerve; by comparison, the number allocated to the auditory nerve is approximately 32,000. The fact that more than 30 times more brain resource is budgeted for processing visual information than for sound information speaks volumes about the way we function. Perhaps the reason images move us more powerfully than other forms of communication is simply that they are the type of information we are best built to receive.

The implications of tapping into the power of images for use in interpersonal business communication are profound. As Adel Al-Saleh, IBM's general manager of global wireless e-business puts it,

"Images are a natural interface for communication," meaning we don't have to be taught how to absorb images; it comes to us naturally. In a given amount of time, vastly more information can be communicated through images than through speech or text.

The challenge in using images to communicate is that, adept as we are at taking in and processing visual information, we must overcome our lack of built-in tools that would help us efficiently create and communicate images. Unlike speech, which we're biologically equipped to produce, to create images we need some form of technology—a burnt stick, a pen, a paintbrush, or a camera. Therefore, throughout human history, technology and visual communication have gone hand in hand. While in some areas, technology is often accused of complicating business processes, *Going Visual* examines how the use of images actually simplifies and streamlines the interpersonal information flow, because individuals can absorb information in the way that is most natural to them.

> The question to ask is not, "What does this new technology allow us to do?" but rather, "What is it that people have always wanted to do that this technology enables them to do better?"
>
> **—Dr. Rudy Burger, Founding CEO, MIT Media Lab Europe**

To set the stage for our twenty-first-century *Going Visual* success stories, we have assembled a brief history that illustrates how humankind has used technology to communicate with images through the ages. By studying this history, we have identified three basic elements that mark the evolution of visual communication as a useful medium:

PERFORMANCE ELEMENTS OF VISUAL COMMUNICATION

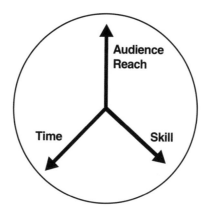

1. *Skill level.* Level of expertise necessary to create an image that communicates.

2. *Time requirements.* How long it takes to create the image.

3. *Audience reach.* How many individuals can view the image.

Elements 1 and 2 determine the cost of creating an image. Element 3 has a direct bearing on the value of that image as a means of communication. This book examines how the value of visual communication has soared, while its cost has fallen dramatically.

As far back as 16,000 to 9,000 B.C., in the Altamira caves of northern Spain, humans used natural pigments like ochre and zinc oxides to paint multicolored pictures on the rock walls. These paintings required a high degree of skill, were created slowly and carefully, and, because of their location, deep in the darkest caves, were viewed by very few people.

The Egyptians and Mayans developed carving technology and skills to render their visual messages in stone. These were very refined, labor-intensive images, created by highly skilled craftsman and viewed only by people who stood before them at the location.

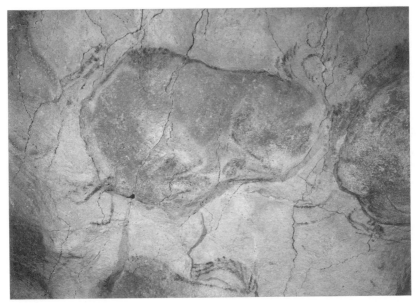

Altamira cave painting

Centuries later, the Western world embraced painting on canvas, wood, and plaster as its means of visual expression. As a visual communication technology, painting, while far superior to what had come before, had severe limitations, as exhibited by reviewing the three performance elements:

1. *Skill level.* The level of skill necessary to create a realistic rendering of a physical reality—a portrait, a landscape, a city scene—was exceedingly high, and only a few individuals practiced the art.

2. *Time requirements.* The time it took to create a painting was typically measured in days, weeks, or even months. Therefore the power of paintings to communicate was the province of very few: the rich, who could afford to commission the creation

Stone carvings at Palenque, Mexico

of images (most often likenesses of themselves and their families), and church and political leaders, who commissioned paintings of religious or historical scenes as part of their exercise of power.

3. *Audience reach.* The physical image itself—the painting—was unique and could be seen only in person, severely limiting the number of people who could be reached by its message.

The advent of silver halide photography in the early 1800s changed the equation. True, the level of skill required to use the

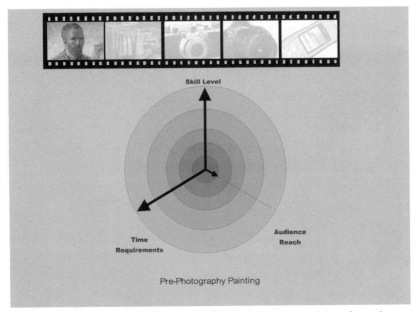

Painting requires a very high level of skill and investment of time from the artist in return for a very limited audience reach.

medium in its infancy was not dramatically lower than was the case for painting. However, photography was a breakthrough in two respects. First, the time required to create an image was distinctly reduced. A picture could be captured in minutes and converted into a viewable reproduction within hours, through a repeatable process. Since time, even then, was money, the effect was to lower the economic barriers to the creation of images, giving birth to the first incarnation of the photography industry—the portrait studios that, for the first time in history, enabled ordinary people to have likenesses of themselves made for posterity. In addition, it also made possible field photography and the chronicling of the Civil War.

Second, an equally important breakthrough was the introduction of the first negative/positive methods that made it possible to reproduce multiple copies of an image. This allowed these images to be distributed for hundreds—and, with the emergence of newspapers, thousands—to see. As a communication technology, early photography enabled the creation of unprecedented numbers of images and gave these images unprecedented reach: No longer confined to the walls of the cave, the church, or the homes of the wealthy, images began conquering the world.

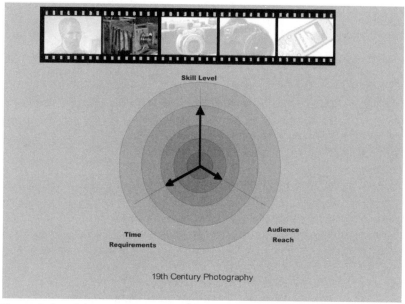

The main breakthrough of nineteenth-century photography was the reduced time to create an image.

The introduction of easy-to-use film cameras in 1900, epitomized by the Kodak Brownie and the slogan, "You press the button, we'll do the rest," began democratizing image capture. A picture could be captured in less than a second, by a person with modest skills, and printed very inexpensively using mass-production machines. The great illustrated magazines—*Life, Look,* and others—that came into being as a result of this technology made images an integral part of the mass-market culture.

The second half of the twentieth century saw further progress in imaging technology, including the emergence of highly sophisticated automatic still-image cameras and the use of analog video in camcorders and VCRs. Video became accessible to the mass culture, and the use of still images exploded. Today, more than 150 years into the evolution of silver halide photography, anyone who can look through a viewfinder and press a button can get an excellent picture, an hour later have prints, and within a week distribute them to people around the world for just a few dollars.

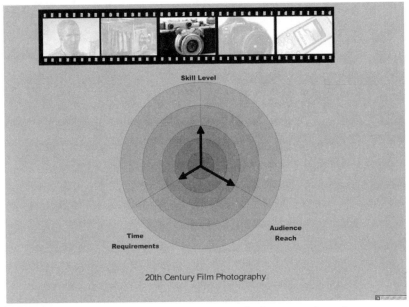

In the twentieth century, film-based photography became a broadly accessible consumer activity.

Just as silver halide photography reached its apex, a newer form of imaging appeared on the scene. In the early 1990s, digital technology changed the game forever by turning both still and video images into electronic bytes.

Digital photography is instantaneous by its very nature, compressing the time required for producing an image to virtually zero.

Since no consumables are used other than battery power, the incremental cost of each image is also essentially zero. Furthermore, the ability to add "intelligence" to digital products has enabled engineers to advance their craft to the point that digital cameras and photoquality printers are now so smart, so automatic, that almost anyone can operate one and get pleasing results. As Nikon vice president Jerry Grossman put it, "We're at the point where the camera does all the work, and so we're seeing more and more nonphotographic people coming into photography." Moreover, the merging of still and video technology is occurring rapidly. Most digital still cameras capture video clips, and many videocams are capable of taking still photos.

The biggest advance resulting from the advent of digital photography, however, is in the global reach that this new technology platform has afforded for visual communication. As a consequence of being captured in a digital format, images have gained entry to the staggeringly large and powerful network of computing, the Internet, and telecommunications resources that have been built up over the past 20 years.

It turns out that the overhype, overinvestment, and overdevelopment of the dot-com craze has had the positive, lasting effect of providing a sophisticated infrastructure to enable the next generation of interpersonal communications. While many of the dot-bombs can be ascribed to bad or nonexistent business models, the passion behind much of the technological development reflected genuine needs and desires to communicate in new, instant, ever-connected ways. A digital image can be captured and transmitted virtually anywhere on earth and distributed to hundreds of thousands of people in an instant. This combination of inexpensive, easy-to-use devices and the burgeoning worldwide information network means that the richness of visual communication is no longer restricted only to media conglomerates, but can be employed by anyone with an Internet connection. This represents a

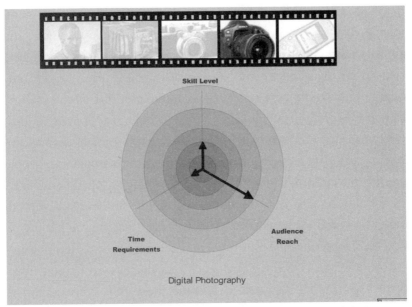

Digital Photography

Now that the technology has matured and come down in price, digital photography makes picture taking even more accessible.

true technology-driven democratization of information, opening the door for *Going Visual.*

The most recent chapter in the history of visual communication technology began in 2003, when digital cameras merged with cell phones to produce the camera phone—the fastest-growing consumer product in history. By 2006, it is estimated that there will be 60 million camera phones in use in the United States.

Camera phones offer the simplest possible form of instant image capturing—simply push a button. In addition, they provide a direct connection to the wireless network—simply push another button to transmit the image.

More important, camera phones have created a historic sociological change in the way visual communication can fit into our lives. People tend to carry their cell phones with them wherever they go. They have become, along with our wallet and our keys, an item we

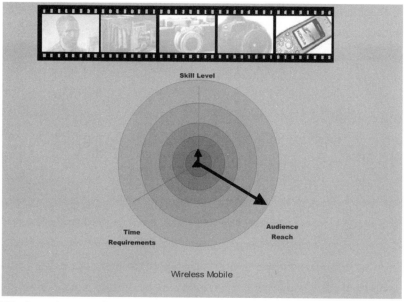

Wireless photography marries imaging to the global reach of the Internet.

automatically take with us when we leave home. Given that these cell phones will, in very short order and with very few exceptions, all have built-in cameras (today you would be hard-pressed to find a camera-less cell phone for sale in Japan) we are rapidly evolving toward a society whose every member is equipped with an image-capturing device during all their waking hours, wherever they are. What's more, because the cell phone is by nature a connected device, images that are captured instantly can be just as instantly transmitted through the network, potentially reaching millions. In that sense, the camera phone is not so much a merger of the camera and the telephone as it is a merger of the camera and the global telecommunications infrastructure. Imaging is thus intimately and inextricably linked to the mainstream of human connectedness, allowing all of us to communicate in ways we have only imagined until now. *Going Visual* aims to spark your imagination.

A decade ago the technology at the disposal of a white-collar lifestyle would typically have included a hardwired phone, a fax, a calculator, a typewriter, and possibly a computer for spreadsheets and word processing. Coupled with the power of digital images, today's tools—computers, printers, cell phones, personal digital assistants (PDAs), the Internet, and e-mail—are defined by their dynamic portability and enable new communication possibilities for virtually any businessperson. The computer has evolved from a deskbound, number-crunching calculator into a laptop center of business information and communication. The early years of the twenty-first century have ushered in the arrival and mass adoption of an array of mobile devices, such as PDAs and smart camera phones, in which computer and communication functions are built into tiny, mobile packages connected to worldwide networks. It's difficult today to find any businessperson without an e-mail address. This was unthinkable a decade ago. Ten years from now our reliance on laboriously translating what we see—that is, visible information—into words rather than communicating with images will be equally unthinkable.

During our wide-ranging conversations with leading business-people, technologists, educators, artists, financial analysts, and others who are shaping the future of communication in the digital age, we encountered a striking degree of agreement that, with respect to the evolution of visual communication tools, a tipping point has been reached between skills, economics, and usability, and as a result mass adoption is not only possible, it is inevitable. For the first time in human history, we can capture and transmit an image across the globe in mere seconds. This is a quantum shift in human interconnectedness, and its power is available to anyone who reads this book. Kodak's Jim Stoffel observed, "I think that if you look at how technology has made it easier to capture important information like personal moments, that same thesis applies directly to business. If you have a camera with you on a business trip, you'll capture important information about that trip. Just as we plan and execute picture taking around a birthday, we should learn to plan and execute in the same way around our travels and our everyday experiences, because clearly that's important in our business experiences. I went down to Washington recently, calling on various senators, and one of them carries his digital camera all the time because he's going to meet a ton of people during his day and many times he wants to remember the person who has something to show him and he just snaps a picture. For that senator, using pictures has clearly migrated from his personal life to his business life. There are many of us who are experiencing that same thing." Communicating using digital data is expanding at such a rapid pace that, as Gail Whipple, vice president of Global Digital Media at IBM notes, "More electronic information has been created in the last two years than in all previous history. Electronic storage is now cheaper than paper storage. That wasn't true two years ago, but it is now." Because businesses have gone digital, the jump to *Going Visual* is a logical one, and Whipple declares, "Any company of any size can use visual media." The ability to exercise that power by building it into everyday business processes is now a key differentiator for any enterprise—a differentiator between those who will succeed because their communication processes are fast, unambiguous, and inclusive, and those who will remain hobbled by antiquated systems.

In Chapter 2, we present the steps and methods of the *Going Visual* strategy, which offers a practical guide though the integration of visual communication capabilities into an organization's everyday projects, goals, and processes.

A Brief History of Digital Image Capture

In a little more than a decade, since the introduction of the first commercial digital cameras in 1991, these devices have progressed from exotic, very expensive, highly complex instruments to a ubiquitous, inexpensive, and simple part of our daily lives.

In 1991, a 1.3-megapixel CCD (1,024 × 1,280 pixels), manual-focus black-and-white camera with a hardwired 200-megabyte external hard disk drive, monocolor display, and a total weight of 55 pounds cost $30,000. It was the first commercial digital camera, introduced by Kodak.

In 1994, Apple Computer released the Quicktake 100. It captured a VGA (640 × 480 pixels) resolution image and had 1 megabyte of internal memory. Its list price was $739. This camera produced images whose quality was certainly no match for film, but its introduction nevertheless marked the moment when digital photography began its ascent in the mass-consumer market.

Throughout the 1990s, camera manufacturers relentlessly improved the image quality and ease of use of these devices to make them attractive to the average person. On a parallel track, computer operating systems became more image-friendly—capable of transferring images to the computer and storing them once they were there. Software for editing, viewing, managing, sharing, and integrating images into documents was also developed with the consumer in mind. Digital photography went mainstream.

By 2004, digital camera capability had improved dramatically, while prices fell to mass-consumer levels. A typical 3-megapixel CCD weighing approximately 6 ounces and measuring 4.3 × 2.7 × 1.5 inches has a retail price of less than $200.00. (A *megapixel* is equal to 1 million *pixels*, or picture elements, a measure of the clarity of an image. A 3-megapixel camera would be more than sufficient for most on-screen uses and produce good-quality 8" × 10" prints. As of this writing, most inexpensive consumer digi-

(Continued)

(Continued)

tal cameras feature 3 to 5 megapixels.) Memory cards holding up to 2 gigabytes of data are available for pennies per megabyte. Cameras like the one shown here are capable of also capturing video and sound clips and support fully automatic exposure settings for virtually any type of lighting or scene. These cameras automate the image transfer process through the use of wired and wireless connections and printing doc stations. Eastman Kodak's Dale McIntyre put the new devices and software in this context, "In today's work flow, the consumer only has to

want, the system does." Manufacturers now produce lines of sub-$1,000 digital cameras, which are equal to, and in some cases exceed, the capabilities of film. And these capabilities are constantly growing while prices continue to decrease.

In 2003, wireless phones featuring embedded, full-color digital cameras and high-speed, wireless Internet access were introduced into the U.S. market. In 2004, 9 million were in use in the United States, and by 2006 we project that 20 percent of our population, or 60 million people, will be carrying camera phones. Early models captured VGA (640 × 480 pixels) images, and camera phones have quickly evolved to 2, 3, and even 5 megapixels with flash, zoom, and video-capture features. Some have smart-phone features, with built-in Internet browsers, date and address books, word and spreadsheet programs, and MP3 music players. They enable users to take pictures or videos and send them by e-mail to another phone or to any e-mail address. Taking and sending a picture takes mere seconds, which led LightSurf's Philippe Kahn to call the camera phone "an instant visual-communication device." The camera option was introduced as a $100 add-on to the phone, but quickly, due to the huge worldwide demand for these devices, has become an essentially free upgrade.

We see this same diminution of cost and complexity taking place across the board in imaging devices: Video cameras, which 15 years ago cost thousands of dollars, can now be had for hundreds of dollars and used by schoolchildren. Surveillance cameras can now be purchased for less than $100 and can be deployed easily. Now that the traditional barriers to technology adoption—prohibitive price and difficulty of use—have been virtually eliminated, the core issue for a businessperson to resolve is, "Why should I adopt a visual communication strategy for my business?"

PRACTICAL EXERCISE

If you had a camera with you during the workday you could take a picture of:

A work group	A customer
A piece of equipment	An employee
A product	A production line
A whiteboard	A part
A document	A building
A drawing	A room
A display	A mechanical detail
A location	An architectural detail
Your place of business	A physical detail

A procedure
An object
An article of clothing
A color
A shape
A moment in time
A fabric
A criminal
An accident scene
A suspect

A victim
Something you're building
Something you're tearing down
Something you're fixing
Something you want to buy
Something you want to sell
Something you own
Something you're insuring
Someone you meet
Yourself

The Four Essential Requirements and Five Action Steps of a *Going Visual* Strategy

The *Going Visual* strategy we present in the following pages comes from our close study of innovative businesses, large and small, simple and complex, that have reaped significant benefits by transforming their interpersonal business communications from words alone into an image-rich mix. We looked for patterns in the ways these companies went from text to image and distilled those into an action plan that any business can implement. The plan has two elements:

1. The *business case* establishes the *four essential requirements* by which a business sets the goals and measures the effectiveness of deploying a *Going Visual* strategy.

2. The *process* consists of *five action steps* that serve as guiding principles for planning and implementing a *Going Visual* strategy.

THE BUSINESS CASE: FOUR ESSENTIAL REQUIREMENTS

Going Visual is about changes—changes in the way we think about and create information, changes in interpersonal communication, and changes in the way we use technology. Basic to implementing these changes in a business environment is that they must be justified by yielding significant enhancement of the organization's goals and functions. With so many technology choices that modern businesspeople have to make, we knew it was important to ask the most important questions that arise when making the decision to adopt new technologies and techniques.

The answers came from Vyomesh Joshi, executive vice president of Hewlett-Packard's imaging and printing group, the man who launched HP's very successful digital-imaging strategy more than 10 years ago and continues to lead it today. One question, he told us, is so critically important that he thinks about it every day: How do you go from data to decision? In this era of information overload, how do we use our eyes and brain to make decisions?

"If you think about how you go from data to information knowledge," Joshi said, "more and more, that knowledge needs to be personalized. It's all about what is important to me, the user. When I think about the use model, the technology has to appeal to the person who is driving the creation of information. The devices will have to become personal, as will the data we are linking so we can move from information to knowledge, and have that 'digital conversation' we are all striving for."

Joshi said that, on a broader level, he views three imperatives as critical to moving a business to adopt any new technology:

1. Knowledge-worker productivity must be increased.

2. Decision-making support must be enhanced.

3. Customer loyalty must be promoted.

These are bedrock concepts whose effect on an organization is measurable. The detailed business examples in the pages that follow illustrate how employing a *Going Visual* strategy accomplishes all three of these objectives and how, in our accelerated digital information age, that strategy is essential to establishing and maintaining a competitive edge. We also discovered a fourth imperative that is required for an entire organization to embrace and adopt *Going Visual:*

4. New technology must enhance the overall values and mission of the organization.

We have seen countless cases where new technology is brought into an organization and has little or no beneficial effect because, as it turned out, its adoption ran against the grain of the organization's business culture. In our explorations we always kept in mind that our interest was not in technology for technology's sake—that never works—but in human interaction through communication, first and foremost. As Phil Garrison, vice president of subscriber equipment at Sprint put it when asked why people adopt and stick with new technology, "These things have to solve some basic drive that a customer has; they've got to solve problems. If you don't solve something that's really useful for customers, and it's just interesting, you tend to get the people that flow through and try every gadget; they come and they go. You've got to give them performance and an acceptable price/value relationship." If a company's culture embraces good communication as an important core value, then adopting a *Going Visual* strategy becomes critical. All the stories that follow make the good-for-business case, first and foremost.

COMMUNITIES OF INTEREST

One of the organizing principles in researching *Going Visual* was to identify the Community of Interest for each of the businesses in our case studies, a concept that defines the universe of a given business's communications flow. All businesses operate in Communities of Interest, the interest being commerce. Who makes up your community? The people and organizations you interact with to conduct business. For example, if your business is retail sales, your community will obviously include your customers, the manufacturers who supply you with products, and your own employees. In addition, it would also include the delivery companies you use, your landlords, your financial institutions, the people who design and place your advertising, your industry peers, and possibly more, depending on the nature of your business. If you were a wedding and party planner, your community could include: your clients, hotels, churches, and other facilities, florists, caterers, clothing designers, bands, ministers, rabbis, and priests—all the people with whom you exchange information in the course of doing your job. You get the picture.

In our examples, we examine how Communities of Interest begin to work in image-centric ways when people begin to think visually—and how the larger and more complex the Community of Interest becomes, the greater the benefits of *Going Visual.*

We also show how images have a unique power not just to convey information, but also to build unity and consensus around that information and to promote action and decision making throughout a community. Because images are complete and detailed and deliver an information experience that has greater impact than words, a common base of visual information proves to be the most efficient form of shared experience from which to make decisions. The communities we explore in the following chapters range from a sales rep's relatively simple community of 150 manufacturers and clients to an intricate web of thousands of diverse members in the case of an outdoor advertising company.

We also found that, because images are such a rich form of communication, and because they can be instantly created and quickly transmitted through the network, some visual communication redefines lines of reporting by taking a more direct route from sender to decision maker than a text document might. The very nature of communicating by e-mail and the Internet has shifted the dynamic of interpersonal relationships from one based essentially on one-to-one phone calls and letters to, with the simple click of the "cc" button, a group experience, extending the audience reach that we spoke of in Chapter 1. This is a crucial driver for communicating instantly through a Community of Interest. As you will see in Chapter 3, images showing the progress of a construction project can, for example, be sent directly from a field supervisor to all the decision makers who need to sign off on it, saving time and money by accelerating the decision-making process. The Community of Interest is the bloodstream of any business.

THE FIVE ACTION STEPS TO *GOING VISUAL*

Going Visual is about communications, and the concept of a Community of Interest is integral to analyzing a business's communication flows, which makes identifying your Community of Interest fundamental to the first of our five action steps: the *survey.*

Step 1. Survey: Identify Your Community of Interest and Recognize Wherever an Image Could Replace Words

Do an inventory of your internal and external business communications. Identify all the participants in your Community of Interest, and look for instances of written or verbal information that might be significantly improved if replaced or augmented by images.

To visualize your own community of interest, Ted Wilson, an HP Fellow in the imaging and printing group, suggests: "Think of your workaday life, and try to mark the separate groups or Communities of Interest that you interact with in an ordinary day. You'll find that it's quite a varied group, and at first glance you might overlook some that you deal with on an ongoing, long-term basis, precisely because that's become routine." Defining your community is an ongoing process that evolves as you *Go Visual.*

Next, it's important to allow yourself to imagine: *What if?* What if people in your organization could *show* their colleagues something they need to visualize—a location, an object, or a physical condition—instead of describing it to them in words? What if you yourself could actually see what a colleague is trying to describe to you? How dramatically would that improve the quality of your everyday communication and your effectiveness at your job? How would that improve your decision-making process? From that general understanding, you can then move on to specifics.

- Which individuals or departments should *go visual?*

- Which documents or communications would this most effectively enhance?

- What specific information is going to evolve from text to image?

- What is the purpose of the communication?

- Who creates the initial information?

- Who receives the information?

- How is the information used and reused?

- How is the information distributed?

- How is the information stored?

- How does adding images fit into the existing information flow?

- What price point makes implementation of a *Going Visual* strategy feasible?

Going Visual is not a one-time, all-or-nothing proposition; rather it is an evolution wherein the most obvious opportunities are addressed first. A key effect of the initial implementation is the uncovering of other areas that would benefit from *Going Visual.* The preceding list enables you to identify those low-hanging fruit that will yield clear, immediate benefits.

Step 2. Implement Capture and Viewing Processes

Equip the appropriate senders and recipients of communications who are Going Visual *with the necessary imaging technology, and train them to use it effectively.*

In this phase you will begin putting *Going Visual* into practice, which requires you to identify and obtain some equipment. As you will see in the stories that follow, the equipment could be as simple as one capture device and a printer or as complex as several hundred of them. Here are some of the questions you need to ask:

- What specific information can best be described in images? Will still images suffice, or is video necessary?

- Will the images be viewed only, or will they need to be printed?

- Will the images be discarded after use or stored? (We recommend planning to store them, even if you're not initially sure how that might be useful.)

- What hardware is needed to fulfill the preceding requirements?

- What software is needed?

- Having developed a basic equipment specification, you will also need to address human factors.

- What is the technical ability of the typical person who will be creating the content? What kind of training, if any, will the person need?

Depending on how the images are used after capture, you may have to ask similar questions regarding the people who will view and/or store the images.

Now it's time to take the initial step—and *go visual.*

Step 3. Design and Implement an Image Archive

Create a resource that provides access, retrieval, and storage of the images.

An image archive is a dedicated digital storage area where images can be saved in an organized, systematic way. As you will learn, in the early stages of a *Going Visual* implementation there may be a trickle of images, but as the value of images expands their use throughout the Community of Interest, that trickle becomes a stream, and organizing an archive becomes essential. Our experience is that, in the vast majority of cases, visual information turns out to be more valuable down the road than you anticipate at the outset, so we recommend that you do some degree of archiving—even if it is as simple as preserving the images on CDs with date ranges and project labels. We examine archiving in depth in Chapter 6, "Smart Images: Making Images Work Systematically Over Time." Here are six questions you should ask in establishing an archive:

1. What are the purposes of the archive?

2. Who has access to the archive? Who authorizes access to the archive?

3. Where does the archive reside? Should it be in-house? If so, where? Or should you go the outsourcing route?

4. What information will be used to search and access the archive?

5. How large does the initial archive need to be to accommodate the number of files and their file sizes you expect to be creating?

6. How will the archive grow, both physically (how will you add storage?) and organizationally (who will be in charge of monitoring

your archive space and specifying, buying, and installing the necessary upgrades)?

Step 4. Track and Evaluate

Observe and analyze the effectiveness of the Visual Communication strategy in terms of the four essential requirements: increased knowledge-worker productivity, a better and faster decision-making process, the promotion of customer loyalty, and the enhancement of the overall values and mission of the organization.

As mentioned earlier, *Going Visual* is an evolving process. The more you do it, the better you get at it, and the more instances you find where it can benefit you. Use the following four guidelines to evaluate your progress, based on our set of principles for successful technology adoption.

1. *Increasing knowledge-worker productivity.* This measure of success examines whether workers who have gone visual are in fact creating visual data that, by virtue of its information-rich nature, is more accurate, unambiguous, and specific and authored in less time with consistently positive results than was previously possible with text or voice only. The key questions are:
    *   Does the use of images reduce the number and complexity of communications that must be sent in order to make a point?
    *   Does the use of images reduce the number of errors caused by miscommunication?
    *   Has the creation and use of images become a natural, everyday reflex?

- How have the people who are now creators of visual content progressed in their ability to think and communicate visually?

2. *Enhancing decision-making support*

   - Are the images being captured and viewed speeding the process of getting workers and executives to move from raw information to decision?

   - Is a consensus being reached in a more streamlined and effective manner as a result of everyone in the decision-making chain seeing the same information instead of reading or hearing words that they must interpret visually for themselves?

3. *Promoting customer loyalty*

   - Are customers expressing greater satisfaction with respect to their interactions with you?

   - When visual information is distributed to clients, do they find it to be an improvement in the process? Are they reporting that the images add to the value delivered to them?

   - Does *Going Visual* appear to have created a competitive advantage for you?

4. *Enhancing the overall values and mission of the organization.* To a significant extent, positive results in the previous three categories provide reliable confirmation that the organization's values and mission have genuinely been enhanced. However, the following additional dimensions are useful to examine as well:

   - Do images improve communication and interpersonal relationships within the organization and the Community of Interest? In other words, does the use of images, by reducing the number of miscommunications and errors, help people get along better with each other and feel more like a team?

- At a time when society demands significantly more transparency in business transactions, does *Going Visual* provide the method to produce the most accurate, meaningful, and accessible activity records possible?

Step 5. Reassess and Educate

Having identified the areas of greatest gains, invest in them further to maximize benefits to the organization. Keep abreast of emerging visual technologies, and evaluate how those technologies could solve additional business problems.

Going Visual is a process of discovery, experimentation, and change. As the stories that follow unfold, you will learn how individuals and organizations progress from entry level to expert visual communicators. In every case we studied, the more images are used, the more uses the Community of Interest finds for them. At this stage it is important to take stock and ask these questions:

- What has the organization learned about *Going Visual?*

- What barriers and limitations have been encountered?

- What new technology and techniques would help overcome those limitations?

- Who else in the organization should go visual?

- What are the next steps in the rollout of the *Going Visual* strategy?

In the following chapters, we introduce you to some of the companies from whom, by observing and analyzing their experiences, we have learned the principles just outlined, and we describe in detail how they have gone visual.

These companies began their transition with little or no imaging experience; they were starting from scratch, using consumer-level, off-the-shelf devices available to anyone. Because these businesses had no peers who had gone visual before them, the process usually began by serendipity, when one person within the company—a field supervisor, a salesperson, a CEO—had a lightbulb moment in which the notion of using a picture instead of a thousand words seemed like an idea worth trying. Sometimes the effort is under the radar until it proves its value and spreads throughout the organization. As Phil McKinney of HP observed, "It's still fairly early. And to be quite honest, if you look at some of the early examples, it isn't corporate-endorsed. It's some guy out there who bought a camera phone, doing it on his own. Sometimes they stumble onto a valuable application by accident. We've seen some successful stealth applications inside the enterprise." One picture led to another, as the images proved far more effective than words alone in communicating specific, often complex information. The organizations at large took notice, and processes began by which the people who knew the most about what information would be best served by *Going Visual,* the communicators themselves, began thinking visually and implementing their own versions of how using images could improve their business processes. This evolution was possible because the skills and tools necessary for success, which not long ago were available only to experts, are now at a level that anyone could master. Amir Majdamehr, Microsoft's corporate vice president of digital media spoke about empowering individuals to go visual: "In the past, when companies wanted to do audio and video they would set up A/V departments, but that went out of favor because it was so expensive to maintain and very few organizations could afford it. We said, 'Why don't we go directly to the people who have the need to do this work, the knowledge workers who need to be effective communicators.' Whether it's the sales force, the marketing department, human resources, or the CEO of a company, they all need to communicate. It was important that the technology be very easy to use, because typically businesspeople don't have the time to learn new skills."

During our conversations with imaging industry executives, some told us personal image-use stories that perfectly caught the essence of *Going Visual.* Bryan Lamkin, senior vice president for digital imaging and video at Adobe Systems and a longtime champion of the democratization of images, related one such story: "In my personal life, just in day-to-day experience, I rarely go out shopping without a camera. If I'm going to the hardware store and I want to get a fitting to fit a certain plumbing device I have at home, it's a lot easier for me just to show them a picture of that on the camera than it is to worry about describing the thing. If I go to Fry's or Best Buy and see our product displays, and I have a problem about how things are being merchandised, I snap a picture and e-mail it to my organization and say, 'Hey let's take a look at this. How do we get this fixed?' Whether I am at a trade show, documenting competitive products, or I want to send compliments back to the team on our booth layout and how well executed that was, I use images. Typically we're used to seeing images as a complementary form of communication, where I'm writing a report and I'll put in a couple of images to enhance that report. I think we are seeing that get turned on its head right now. When I send off the 12 images that I think capture the experience, the text is going to complement the images, instead of vice versa."

It is revealing to look at typical text communications and ask, "How long does it take to write hundreds of words describing an object, a place, a scene, a person?" It could take minutes or hours. In contrast, capturing an image takes a fraction of a second, and then, because it is in digital form, it can immediately be transmitted and communicated to its intended audience. On the receiving end, how long does it take to read a written report? Minutes? Hours? How long does it take to look at an image? Seconds. Which type of communication is most likely to get attention and evoke a response? In the success stories that follow, images proved to be more accurate, more compelling, and more action-provoking than words alone had ever been.

We delved deep to learn how many ways images became valuable to each of these businesses. We examined how the interpersonal relationships within each became organized into Communities of Interest, and how important understanding one's community is to *Going Visual.* We asked how the use of images helped people do their jobs better, and how the simple act of thinking visually and carrying and using a digital camera or camera phone during the business day profoundly changed the way these companies communicate. We examined the effect that images have on those who receive them, and how that impacts the decisions that are made. These are not stories about the occasional e-mailing of images, but about a transformation in communication resulting in images being used as information in many basic business functions.

These personal accounts do not focus on the technical side of imaging, computers, networks, or telecommunication, but rather on the human and practical side of using the technology. Businesses are built on communication between people. The stories will reveal that when the exchange of information is transformed from text to image, extraordinarily useful changes take place that improve the quality of interpersonal relationships and the effectiveness of the communication.

It was fascinating to find that, because images are such a natural medium, the transition from pure text to a blend of image and text was natural as well. In every case, we found that once a company started *Going Visual,* it never looked back.

In our first business story, involving the property management firm Hyder & Company, we dig deeply into each of the elements of our action plan to establish the *Going Visual* approach, wherein images transform the interpersonal communications throughout the Community of Interest. In the chapters that follow, we present the five steps and the four essential requirements in a more narrative structure that allows the voices of the businesspeople who adopted *Going Visual* strategies to personally explain what they did and how they did it.

PRACTICAL EXERCISE

- Start being visually aware. If you don't carry a camera with you, begin to keep track of the times throughout your day when an image might be helpful in communicating something, either as a creator or a viewer.

- If you do not have or do not want to invest in a digital camera, buy a pocket-size single-use film camera and carry it with you during your business day. Think visually and snap a picture of something you want to remember or something you're going to have to describe to someone.

- Take a picture of yourself and store it on your computer. Next time you have to meet someone you've never met, attach it to an e-mail so that person can recognize you. It takes the tension out of searching through a crowd for the right person.

A Tale of Two Meetings

During our extensive field research for this book, we met with many busy people. We'd get together in all kinds of places: offices, hotels, coffee shops, trade shows, airports, or taxis, wherever it happened to be convenient. Early in the process, two meetings taught us a simple yet profound lesson about our own subject, *Going Visual*.

Meeting number one was scheduled to take place at 11:30 A.M. in the lobby of a hotel in New York City. We were getting together for lunch with a literary agent who we hoped would be interested in representing this book. Neither of us had previously met her, so we were standing in the lobby trying to be identifiable, trying to look like two guys waiting for an agent. By 11:50, no one had approached us. Unfortunately, we didn't have the agent's cell phone number and she didn't have ours, so we went to the front desk to see if there was a message. There was, she had called and was running a bit late. We waited another 15 minutes, watching anxiously as women entered the lobby and passed us by until we decided to go into the restaurant and get a table. The restaurant had an open plan so all the tables were visible from the hostess's desk.

She must have looked in when we were peeking at the menu, because we never saw her. We missed her completely. She later told us that when she stood at the hostess's desk she saw a dozen tables with two guys sitting and talking and there was no way she was going to go from table to table trying to figure out who we were, so she left. Meeting missed. Hours wasted. Nerves frayed. Mission not accomplished!

Meeting number two was arranged by phone from Japan. We were speaking to representatives of a Japanese imaging company, and it was decided we'd meet at their booth at a giant trade show in the United States. While we were on the phone, these men, whom we hadn't met, snapped photos of themselves with a digital camera and e-mailed the picture to us. Wanting to be polite, and recognizing a good idea when we saw one, we did the same.

Weeks later, when we entered the convention hall crowded with thousands of people, we confidently walked right up to the familiar faces of our colleagues. Mission accomplished!

The difference between success and failure was simple: a *picture.* We've now made it standard practice to exchange pictures with anyone we're going to meet for the first time.

CHAPTER 3

Putting *Going Visual* into Practice

The company profiled in the following pages successfully deployed a *Going Visual* strategy that began with the purchase of a single consumer-level digital camera, which progressed to 5 and then to 50 cameras. Virtually everyone in this 130-member organization benefited significantly from *Going Visual*. Showing, instead of telling, became the key to making this enterprise more efficient, more effective, and more competitive.

We were drawn to Hyder & Company, a facilities management firm overseeing 52 affordable housing sites located in a several-hundred-mile radius around San Diego County, California, because the core of its story—how an organization can effectively manage a complex matrix of employees in the field, remote facilities, and client and stakeholder relationships—is so fundamental that its lessons can be applied broadly to many types of businesses. By the end of this chapter the reader will find it hard to imagine how Hyder & Company could ever go back to the way it communicated before *Going Visual*.

Dennis Dillon, at the time of our research, Hyder's chief field supervisor, designed and deployed the company's *Going Visual* strategy. Dillon combined his strong background in the practical realities of day-to-day property management with a creative inquisitiveness about new, information-age technology. He identified a critical need to vastly improve the way Hyder gathered and distributed an ever-increasing torrent of data. He reasoned that if a picture is worth 1,000, or even 200 words, it would describe the real-world situations his company constantly dealt with better than words alone had ever done. His goal was to use images to transform the company's traditional, rather dull, time-consuming, text-laden report structure into an image-enhanced, streamlined, dynamic, engaging, detail-rich communication platform. Dillon employed an intuitive yet systematic method in building a strategy that applied *Going Visual*'s five key steps:

1. *Survey.* Dillon performed an inventory of internal and external communications, searching for instances of written or verbal communication that might be significantly improved if replaced or augmented by images.

2. *Implement.* He equipped the appropriate senders and recipients of those communications with the necessary imaging technology and trained them to use it effectively.

3. *Archive.* He created a repository of accessible records of the images for permanent storage and retrieval.

4. *Track and evaluate.* He and his team observed and analyzed the effectiveness of their *Going Visual* strategy as measured against the goals of increased knowledge-worker productivity, better and faster decision-making processes, the promotion of customer loyalty, and the enhancement of the overall values and mission of the organization.

5. *Reassess and educate.* Having identified the areas of greatest gains, Hyder & Company invested in them further to maximize benefits to the organization.

HYDER & COMPANY PROFILE

Hyder & Company, founded in 1970, has flourished for more than 30 years by guaranteeing to a diverse set of property owners that the management, maintenance, and tenant relations required under their contracts were being performed in a high-quality, consistent

Typical Hyder housing site

manner. The company's mission statement puts the importance of communication front and center:

> In order to deliver the highest quality product possible we established a policy of immediate accessibility for our owners. These open lines of communication are the foundation of our success. There is no substitute for personal knowledge and contact with our clients. This is our true competitive edge!
>
> —Hyder & Co. Mission Statement

For the first three decades of Hyder's existence, virtually all the internal and external communication was text-only. The company's initial implementation of a *Going Visual* strategy gave field supervisors the power to visually document the physical conditions at the 52 affordable housing sites it manages. Using these images to show (with pictures) rather than to tell (with text) has redefined the "accessibility" and "open lines of communication" proclaimed in Hyder's mission statement. In the words of Dennis Dillon, "*Going*

Visual allowed us to take our eyes out to the projects anytime we want to. In our field, property management, there will be some very fundamental changes in business practices because of digital photography." We examine these changes and discuss how the lessons learned by Hyder—a company with no previous imaging expertise—apply to businesses in various fields.

STEP 1. SURVEY

Do an inventory of internal and external corporate communications for instances of written or verbal information that might be significantly improved if replaced or augmented by images.

Which Individuals or Departments Should Go Visual?

The first step in answering that question is to identify the company's Community of Interest, the individuals and enterprises with whom it communicates while conducting its daily affairs, and then envision how images could help that community communicate better. Dennis Dillon defined Hyder's Community of Interest as one that includes an *internal* group—field supervisors, site managers, staff, and upper management—and an *external* group—property owners, tenants, building and maintenance contractors and other suppliers of products and services to the properties, and various government oversight agencies.

What Information Would Most Effectively Be Enhanced by *Going Visual*?

Dillon examined the communication content and distribution patterns throughout Hyder's Community of Interest and focused on the information produced by a key group of Hyder employees—the five field supervisors who visited the various housing sites to view their condition and to initiate the decision-making processes relating to maintenance, repairs, construction, and owner-tenant relations. All major decisions concerning management of the properties were based on text-only reports generated by these supervisors, whose job essentially consisted of translating what they saw into words. These reports were ideal candidates to go from text to image.

The next step in the survey process is to identify the basic components of the field-report information chain:

- *What information will evolve from text to image?* In this case, written field reports, which primarily describe physical site conditions and recommend actions.

- *What is the purpose of the communication?* To communicate to various members of the Community of Interest the current condition of the properties, to identify physical problems, to initiate action on maintenance and site improvements, and to track progress on projects.

- *Who creates the initial information?* The field supervisors.

- *Who receives the information?* Multiple actors within the Community of Interest.

- *How is the information used and reused?* The Hyder management team studied the reports and made recommendations to the owners. The owners then responded and the projects were initiated. The Hyder team communicated with on-site managers, outside contractors, suppliers, and government inspectors and reported the progress of the projects back to the owners.

- *How is the information circulated?* Through both analog and digital distribution. Some in the community receive printed documents and some receive e-mailed attachments. The Hyder team members also used a combination of print and digital documents to confer with each other.

- *How is the information stored?* At the time of the initial survey, the information archive consisted primarily of paper reports stored in file cabinets at the Hyder headquarters.

- *How does adding images fit into the existing information flow?* Hyder was in the process of equipping all its field supervisors with laptop computers for the creation and distribution of their reports; therefore, that group was equipped to create digital content.

- *What price point makes implementation of a* Going Visual *strategy feasible?* Is this the right time to go visual? Will the strategy pay for itself? Hyder acted on this at the precise time that digital cameras were beginning to come into mass-market price ranges. Those prices have declined steeply, lowering the return-on-investment threshold for future projects.

Having identified the information, the creators and the receivers, Dillon decided to experiment with a modest field trial, using just one digital camera to observe the effect images might have on the communication process. "It was a 1-megapixel model," he explained, "and it worked really well. We passed the camera among our five property supervisors as they went out to their projects so they could take pictures of major construction or safety issues that they wanted to convey either to upper management or to the owners." The supervisors reacted with enthusiasm, discovering that speaking with pictures quickly, accurately, and more effectively communicated their observations and recommendations than did their written reports. Hyder's management and the property owners also were unanimous in their enthusiasm for this new, image-rich reporting technique. Dillon reported, "The decision-making process was greatly enhanced immediately."

Here are three sample photographs taken by Hyder & Company. They aren't artful—but that's the point. These simple images, which anyone could take, convey the equivalent of many pages of tedious text. This is streamlined, content-rich communication.

General condition and landscaping

Graffiti that needs to be painted over

Damage that needs repair

Based on the success of his single-camera survey test, Dillon began projecting how his *Going Visual* strategy would blend into Hyder's overall information infrastructure. "We shared one camera for six months, and then we had the opportunity to upgrade. We were just then going to an all-laptop format for the supervisors so they could have access to company communications through the

Internet and could generate their reports from the field. The images the supervisors were taking had proven so valuable that it made sense at that time to get all of them their own 2.2-megapixel cameras, which were reasonably priced, with more than enough resolution for our purpose."

STEP 2. IMPLEMENT

Equip the appropriate senders and recipients of communications who are Going Visual *with the necessary imaging technology, and train them to use it effectively.*

Given the decision to go forward with a *Going Visual* strategy, a precise matching of the people-skill level to the technological requirements of the mission is key to implementing the initial stages. In Hyder's case, because the employees had no previous imaging experience, the company kept the equipment and software simple and straightforward, making sure its employees would embrace the advantages of using the technology without having to endure a steep learning curve. As with any successful innovation, balancing the benefits and rewards with the effort required to implement the change is critical. If the technology is intimidating and hard to use, that as often as not is a deal breaker. A few basic but core questions help guide the implementation process:

- *What specific information can best be described with images?* In Hyder's case, the physical condition of the properties and the progress of maintenance and construction projects.

- *Will still images suffice, or is video necessary?* At this first stage, still images.

- *What is the technical ability of the typical person who will be creating the content?* The supervisors have no digital imaging experience at all.

- *What hardware is needed to fulfill the requirements?* For each supervisor, one consumer-grade 2.2-megapixel digital camera. A color printer in the office.

- *What software is needed?* The combination of the software provided with the cameras and the computer operating system imaging software is sufficient for this phase.

We asked Dennis Dillon how important a factor ease of use was in deciding which digital camera to buy. He was adamant: "Usability was a huge issue. The cameras we chose have a docking station, which allows you to drop the camera in, push one button, and transfer the files automatically to the computer. It's not, 'Did it get my pictures?' or 'Did it not get my pictures?' Then the camera sits in the docking station, and once the red light is off, the battery is charged—you can grab it and go. Another extremely nice thing about the digital camera is the auto-stamped date. You don't find yourself looking at a picture and saying, 'Gee, when was that taken?' That's a huge benefit. The date function is turned on in all our cameras, so it's always stamped on the image automatically."

Training

When asked how much training was required to get the field supervisors up and running, Dillon said, "Some of them immediately took it up. One of them was really savvy. I just showed him where you plugged the camera in, clicked a couple of settings on his software, and that was it. He never asked me about it again. Some of the other guys were a little bit slower, but once they figured out where the image-transfer button was and what the settings dial did, they were good with it." How many technical-support calls did you get from the field? "You know, after we initially went through how it worked, none." Did they all embrace adding pictures to their work flow? Did they like that idea from the beginning? "Yes, they liked it right away," Dillon said, "because they immediately saw that it would cut down the amount of writing they had to do, and that's a big saving of time and effort."

With some careful planning and basic training, a seamless transition from text-alone to text-plus-image field reports had begun, with the immediate benefit—"saving time and effort"—of increasing productivity.

Everyday Use in the Field

Involving the employees in the survey process introduced the concept of *Going Visual,* as well as some hands-on experience, to Hyder's field supervisors and set the stage for implementation. Bob Dickey, then one of the lead supervisors, enthusiastically described his experience: "I'm not a photographer. I can't really take pictures, but the digital camera makes me a player. It's as easy to use as dialing the phone. The photos don't have to be professional quality; they're documenting the physical problems of the property and how things change. We look at things like landscaping, painting, repairs, and additions. I can take the pictures, then simply download them to my laptop in the field, and then print them out when I return to the office. I now have a six- to eight-month file proof of what's going on. I can e-mail the owners these pictures to enhance the monthly reports we write, which otherwise tend to be pretty boring and dry. I used to have to write a nine-page report describing what I observed; now I just say, 'See picture.' "

The clients are all saying, "We want to see more pictures."

—Bob Dickey

Dickey emphasized how quickly the clients embraced the information-rich elements of images. "Pictures are a big boost in improving the reports and making it unnecessary for the owner to have to travel to the building sites. The clients are all saying, 'We want to see more pictures. They tell us more than your written reports ever did.' Originally, our reports were 40 pages long. Then we trimmed them down to a nine-page form. Using pictures, I can now indicate 'no change,' which means the client can look at the original file picture, or, if there is a change, I say, 'See pictures,' and they can see the condition of the property for themselves without the need for a detailed written report. This has been a really successful thing. Most of the property owners don't live anywhere near their properties, and seeing the pictures has made it possible for them to cut way down on the number of times they have to visit their sites. I have one client who lives 70 miles away from his property and hasn't made a single trip since we started sending him pictures about a year ago."

It's clear from this last statement that by *Going Visual,* by providing information so thorough and compelling, Hyder has significantly increased customer loyalty and level of trust in the company's performance. In the modern business environment, trust is the sharpest competitive edge.

Pulling out their cameras became a natural reflex action for Hyder supervisors. Professor Douglas Ford Ray, photojournalism chair at the Rochester Institute of Technology, in Rochester, New York, explained, "The camera becomes like a pen in your pocket." Instead of reaching for their pens or their keyboards, the Hyder field supervisors are now reaching for their cameras. That's "thinking visually."

Bob Dickey described how often he reaches for his camera. "With the digital camera, I can shoot as many pictures as I want. I can shoot all the details, like getting under the building and following a leaky pipe to find a problem. At the beginning of a project I usually shoot about 30 to 40 pictures, which I then refer to as the standard when doing my reports. I only have to shoot new pictures when there's been a change in condition. On a typical site, each month I'll shoot four to eight pictures. We now use pictures to show contractors problems we need to fix. We have a serious mold situation we're working on right now, and the pictures have been our reference with everybody we've talked to. As the owner of our company says, 'Shoot as many pictures as you want; it doesn't cost us anything.' Also, with the digital camera, I can look at each shot on the screen on the back of the camera and know for sure that I got the picture I need."

The ease with which Dickey describes his image work flow underscores how effectively Hyder integrated the use of images into a text-based system that had been in use for more than 30 years.

Camera Ease of Use Is by Design

It's important to note that the easy-to-use digital cameras employed by Hyder were actually designed for consumers, yet they've found a comfortable home in the business setting. We spoke with Jerry Grossman, a vice president of digital camera maker Nikon, about how important ease of use has become from the camera manufacturer's point of view.

"More and more people who were not previously involved with photography are coming into it," Grossman said. "For us, it's all about making it really simple. We've learned a lot over the last 10 years by studying the way people actually use our cameras, and now we're at the point where the camera does all the work. The fact that these cameras are so easy to use and at such a good price point means a business can buy them for all their employees. Easy to train, easy to buy, it's an easy package to put in your pocket, and your return on investment is going to happen much faster. In most business situations, 2 megapixels is probably enough. You're not blowing the pictures up. You're making small prints. You're storing pictures on a computer, and you're e-mailing them to people. The cost of technically supporting the operator of the camera, which is potentially a really significant business expense, has been taken out of the equation by the 'Keep it simple' mantra."

The success of Hyder's implementation process underscores the importance of:

- Matching the technical requirements of the strategy to the skills of the workforce.

- Training the workforce so they are comfortable enough with the technology to use it enthusiastically.

- Providing value both to the creator of the visual content and the viewer so that the advantages of *Going Visual* are immediate and indispensable, making the change of behavior permanent.

STEP 3. ARCHIVE

Create a resource that provides access, retrieval, and storage of the images.

In the initial launch of a *Going Visual* strategy, the emphasis is often on the immediate benefits of communicating visually. The value of some images may be short-lived, a transitory snapshot that says, "Is this the piece of office furniture I should buy?" or "Is this the correct wiring pattern for this piece of equipment?" These fleeting images may be disposable. In many other cases, the real value of the image is not only as a way to communicate immediate information, but also as a permanent record—in Hyder's case, of the physical condition of a place at a specific time. One measure of an image's value is the number of times it is viewed and the number of uses it has. The images produced by Hyder are viewed by the diverse members of the company's Community of Interest: supervisors, managers, property owners, contractors, inspectors, and tenants. The images may be used many times and integrated into a number of different types of documents: property reports, construction contracts, legal briefs, historical overviews, marketing materials, and interoffice memorandums. There is enormous value in effectively archiving images, along with their supporting documents, so that they can be easily accessed for viewing and repurposing. Creating a strategy to do so is vital.

As described earlier in this chapter, Hyder took a simple, intuitive approach to building its archive. The company viewed the images as extensions of the reports the supervisors had been writing and allowed those individuals to organize and store the data on their individual laptops. This worked well in the first-stage implementation, because the number of images was relatively modest, and only the five supervisors were empowered to capture images. As more images come online from throughout Hyder's vast Community of Interest, and as the use of those images grows ubiquitous, the demands on the archive will increase exponentially. Planning for the future becomes vital. An example of a company with a deep archive that is managed with a sophisticated search-and-retrieval system appears in Chapter 6.

The simple design of Hyder's archive addresses the following questions:

- *What is the purpose of the archive?* To provide an easily accessible visual record of the management activities at each property site.

- *Who has access to the archive?* Hyder's management and field supervisors and, through the monthly reporting and real-time updates, the property owners.

- *Where does the archive reside?* In this stage, on each supervisor's laptop—with plans to transfer the data to a central database.

- *What information is used to search and access the archive?* The images can be found by searching according to site number, date, and property owner.

- *How will the archive grow?* In the first phase of Hyder's Visual Communication strategy, hundreds of images were captured and stored per month. In later stages, that is likely to grow to thousands of images per month. Hyder executives are aware they will have to move the archive from laptops to central servers to meet expanding storage and access needs. In Chapter 6, "Smart Images," we present a company that is adding 27,000 images a month to its archive and has implemented a sophisticated, industrial-strength, distributed, networked storage solution in order to do so.

Instant Accessibility

Once the supervisors were equipped with laptops and digital cameras, they were able to create and store their records electronically and have them with them at all times. This was a huge advance in accessibility to crucial data in comparison to Hyder's old paper-file archives, which were located at the company headquarters and could be accessed only if one physically went there. It was now possible for the supervisors to see and evaluate the visual and written histories of every site and quickly communicate any vital portion of that data to anyone in the Community of Interest. Dennis Dillon describes how the archive has changed: "In the past, the few Polaroid pictures we took never stayed with the actual written nine-page facility-site report; they went into a picture file for the project in a filing cabinet that the clients never saw. That's really cumbersome and ineffective. A lot of times when pictures were needed, we couldn't find them, or we would discover they just hadn't been taken. Now we're much more flexible because we can transmit images through our network digitally, and we can send them to our clients and all of our project sites. Those pictures are stored on each supervisor's laptop, so when they're out at the project the next month for a follow-up, they can refer back to the pictures they took the month before and point out any outstanding issues to the staff in the field."

During this phase of the implementation, each supervisor built his own archive based on his technical expertise. Bob Dickey was very candid: "Some of the other guys are more technical than I am, and more fully use the capabilities of the system. They make more sophisticated documents, but I keep it simple. I print the pictures four or eight to a page." Dickey went on to describe staff meetings held when written reports were the only documentation available. "There are five of us who have to decide how to rate the condition of each property; this is all subjective stuff. With a written report you had to take my word for it, my opinion." When a consensus couldn't be reached on a major expenditure for maintenance or construction because the supervisors felt they had to see the problem for themselves, all five had to take the time to travel to that particular site, trips that could involve hundreds of miles and take an entire workday.

Since *Going Visual,* those trips are no longer necessary because virtually all decisions are made in the regular staff meetings. "We spread the pictures out on the table for everyone to view," Dickey said. "Now we can all see for ourselves what the plumbing or wiring or painting looks like and discuss the ratings based on the same view.

It's really made the process so much better." It is significant to note that the return on investment for the five digital cameras these supervisors use can be credited to the elimination of one of these all-hands site trips.

Dickey described how images have become an important tool in tenant relations: "It is important to have pictures when dealing with renters who have done unauthorized things to the property. We've had cases where people have done horrendous paint jobs on the interior, and, because I now have pictures to back me up, we can proceed against them with great confidence. I haven't had to go to court yet, but I will tell you that when that day comes, and it surely will, knowing we have pictures as evidence will really strengthen our position."

The information-rich, instantly accessible visual archive gives Hyder the ability to:

- Review the *past*. The company can track performance over time and visually verify site conditions for owners and tenants alike.

- Show the *present*. When attached to current site reports or sent in real time, these images can be accessed and instantly repurposed for bids on maintenance or construction projects.

- Store for the *future*. The company can use the images for planning, dispute resolution, marketing, and training.

STEP 4. TRACK AND EVALUATE

Observe and analyze the effectiveness of the Visual Communication strategy in terms of increased knowledge-worker productivity, better and faster decision making, the promotion of customer loyalty, and the enhancement of the overall values and mission of the organization.

Image Information Flow Benefits

How deep does a *Going Visual* strategy reach into an organization? How many ways is Hyder & Company using images? Hyder has created a Community of Interest populated by visually empowered people and organizations. As that network grows, the informational power of the community is multiplied exponentially.

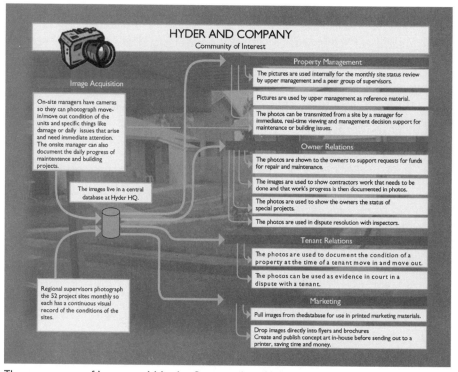

The many uses of images within the Community of Interest

Dennis Dillon reviewed and explained the benefits of 12 key image-use categories he tracks and evaluates:

1. *Regional supervisors photograph the 52 project sites monthly so each has an updated visual record of the site conditions.* "What is most

important is that the more clearly everybody understands the condition of the property, the better off we all are."

2. *The pictures are used internally by upper management and a group of senior supervisors for the monthly site-status reviews.* "Without the pictures, it would be totally impossible to come to a consensus on some major issues without physically taking everybody out to the project to look at it."

3. *The images significantly reduce the number of property-owner site trips.* "It's real peace of mind for the property owners to know that they're getting these pictures every month. They know things are looking all right, that they don't have any major problems. They can drive out on a yearly basis instead of having to go out every quarter."

4. *The pictures are used by upper management as reference material.* "Our CEO, Don Hyder, takes digital photographs of some of the projects and then presents them in our monthly staff meetings as either something that he likes seeing or as something that needs some attention. Also, when Don visits the sites, he's not going to be shocked or dismayed that there is a certain look to a project which he didn't expect, since he's already seen our photographs on a regular basis."

5. *The photos are shown to the owners to support requests for funds for repair and maintenance.* "If there is the need for paint, concrete work, or any other maintenance issue, the owners can actually see it with their own eyes. Getting owners to sign off on replacing a sidewalk or getting a paint job done on a building is a lot easier when they're looking at a picture."

6. *The images are used to show contractors the work that needs to be done, and the progress of the job is then documented in photos.* "A supervisor or site manager will send pictures because they want

Construction in progress   Construction complete

to point out that something really needs to be done. Once the request is approved, those pictures can be sent to contractors for bids, which speeds the process by eliminating the need for extra visits to the site. In some cases, the owner has instructed that something be done, and we want to take a picture of the completed job to show them that we did in fact relandscape this area—here's how it looks now. It's important to send that visual documentation along with the written report so that when we're billed for 20 hours of labor on a repair, we can say to the owner, 'Yes, that looks like 20 hours of repair work,' and then the payment is authorized."

7. *The photos are used to show the owners the status of special projects.*
   "We had an ongoing major maintenance issue having to do with salt damage at one of our projects, and the owner was very concerned but couldn't physically go to the project. It was a huge investment to stop this damage from happening. I started to take a series of pictures every month, and I had a year's worth of photographs so we could track it visually. I could show the owner what the status of the condition was and what steps we were taking to correct the problem."

8. *The photos are used in dispute resolution with inspectors.*
   "Because some of our projects are government supported, we

deal with federal inspectors. For example, I had an inspector come out and claim that we had substantial damage to our roofs, when in fact we were only missing two laminated shingles from one roof. I went to the property, took pictures, and when I responded to the inspector I wrote, 'Per photograph below, only these two shingles were missing.' A written report wouldn't have had the same credibility."

9. *The photos are used to document the condition of a property at the time a tenant moves in and moves out.* "When a tenant moves in, we do a walk-through of the unit during which we document the property visually. This walk-through minimizes the proba- bility of a future dispute, because the tenant observes that not only is this guy writing all this stuff down, he's taking pictures! The process of vacating the property and comparing its condi- tion to the condition at the time of possession is a very big thing in property management, and digital imaging has hardly been used there at all. Over the next few years, because the docu- mentation of the condition of the units will change from a text- only written document to a more graphic format, our business is really going to change."

10. *The photos can be used as evidence in court in a dispute with a ten- ant.* "If you're in a situation where perhaps someone is disput- ing a charge about the *vacate* report or you're evicting somebody because of damages and you end up in court, having a visual reference of the property at the time of the occupant's move-in and move-out is extremely powerful."

11. *The images can be used for training purposes.* "We've had some training issues come up that can be dealt with very simply by using a picture. We had a brand-new piece of equipment, a paint sprayer, that wasn't cleaned properly and was in such bad

What is wrong with this picture?

Maintenance training photo

condition after only one use that I decided to e-mail a picture of it to all the site managers with the simple question: 'What's wrong with this picture?' It was very effective."

12. *Images are used for marketing materials.* "We have this great database of photographs that we can scroll through to see which ones we want to use for marketing purposes, such as preparing a flyer. It cuts down enormously on the amount of time it takes us to get a piece from a concept to a print that's ready to send to a customer. Also, we can do the mock-up in-house and save the money we used to have to pay to the printer."

Summing up, Dillon said, "There are probably a lot of other uses I haven't even thought of yet. In our field, in property management, it's just a matter of time until the use of digital images becomes industry-wide. There will be some very fundamental changes in the way we do business because of digital photography."

Reviewing the Four Essential Requirements

1. *Increasing knowledge-worker productivity.* The measure of success is whether a knowledge worker is able to create visual data that, by virtue of its information-rich nature, is more accurate, more unambiguous, and more specific and is authored in less time with consistently positive results than previously possible with text. The key issues are (1) whether the use of images reduces the number and complexity of communications that must be sent in order to make a point and (2) whether the use of images reduces the number of errors caused by miscommunication.

   Other measures of a successful implementation include: Has the creation and use of images become a natural, everyday reflex? Have the people who are now creators of visual content progressed in their abilities to think and communicate visually? In Hyder's case the adoption of images has passed each of these tests.

2. *Enhancing decision-making support.* Do images speed the process of getting from raw information to making a decision? Can consensus be reached in a more streamlined and effective manner if everyone in the decision-process chain is literally seeing the same information instead of reading or hearing words that they must visualize for themselves? Hyder & Company would answer with a resounding *yes.*

3. *Promoting customer loyalty.* When clients are brought into the imaging information chain do they embrace the value? Hyder's clients unanimously reacted with a call for more pictures because they "learned more from the pictures than [they] ever learned from the written reports." They demonstrated a higher level of trust in the operation, evidenced by fewer physical

visits to the sites. When a company improves its level of client communication, resulting in a dynamic upgrade in the effectiveness of the relationship, that company is staying out in front of the competition.

4. *Enhancing the overall values and mission of the organization.* For a company whose mission statement declares, "Open lines of communication are the foundation of our success," the adoption of image-rich communication is mission-critical. *Going Visual* provides the method for producing the most accurate, meaningful, and accessible activity records possible.

STEP 5. REASSESS AND EDUCATE

Having identified the areas of greatest gains, invest in them further to maximize benefits to the organization. Learn about the application of emerging visual technologies, and evaluate how those technologies could solve additional business problems.

Hyder's successful phase one deployment of a *Going Visual* strategy set the stage for phase two—going from 5 cameras to 50, one at each site. New goals and challenges were addressed by asking some fundamental questions:

- *What has the organization learned about* Going Visual? Once images were introduced into the decision-making process, they became an indispensable tool. The viewers of the content quickly came to expect image-based material, and their harvesting of information from that content became quite sophisticated. Indeed, their reactions functioned as feedback that began to drive the types of images that were created. The viewers realized the power of images and wanted to leverage it for purposes that, in some cases, hadn't been anticipated by the creators. This not only strengthened Hyder's relationships with these viewers, but also improved the overall system. Listening to the needs of the viewer is crucial.

- *What barriers and limitations have been encountered?* As with any form of communication, some people are more effective at it than others. Studying and analyzing the most successful and least successful examples of *Going Visual* is an ongoing process that will help improve the system.

- *What are the next steps in the rollout of the* Going Visual *strategy?* Assessment of the phase one *Going Visual* implementation clearly demonstrated its value, and the next step was clear: Expand the capabilities of the system by providing more individuals with imaging devices and add the necessary computer network storage and software to support more images. Specifically, this meant giving digital cameras to all 52 local site managers, nearly half of the company's 130 employees, and building a central database at company headquarters.

Dennis Dillon expressed his enthusiasm for *Going Visual* this way: "Digital camera prices have come down enough that we're now about to buy units that will stay at each of our 52 sites. The local project managers will be able to transmit images to us so we can see, in near real time, what transpired or what situation the manager has a question about. In our business, time is of the essence, especially when it comes to making decisions at the projects, some of which are over 200 miles away from us, where we need to get approval to spend money from a government agency. Having our eyes out in the field has proved essential."

When it comes to educating these local supervisors about the technology, a trickling down of expertise—from the now experienced field supervisors—will make training merely another part of the suite of skills that the job requires.

A major area of reassessment for Hyder involves archiving. With the success of an image-rich strategy, and with a major expansion planned, the challenge is to manage the thousands of images that all these site supervisors will be generating each year. Storing the images and supporting documents in laptops and computers at the local sites will not suffice. Hyder plans to establish a central database where all the data can be accessed. Dillon is educating himself on how to accomplish this. "We're looking at some management software that has digital photography integrated into it," he says. "I've talked to a number of property-management software development companies, stressing to them that having photo support inherently built into the software is critical."

Another area for improvement is to integrate technology that enables faster transmission of digital photographs over low-bandwidth connections. Said Dillon, "Some of the sites have dial-up connections rather than broadband, and trying to transmit large picture files can take a lot of time at their end. We're in the process of upgrading." Bandwidth becomes particularly important as companies like Hyder begin to incorporate types of visual media that provide even richer information, such as video. "We've talked about using video," Bob Dickey told us. "We've even talked about live video. For instance, if a contractor is out on the site and none of us is close enough to meet him, he could show us a problem in real time and we could make a decision on it right then and there. This is just in the talking stages, but I can see how it could save us a lot of time and trouble."

Solutions to the issues that Dillon and Dickey have identified—real-time remote-location access, software-archiving infrastructure, and image-rich media applications—are explored in depth in later chapters.

PRACTICAL EXERCISE

Try photographing:

* *Work in progress for collaborative problem solving.* Keeping a visual record of a project will add an entirely new dimension to group interaction. Where appropriate, images could be shared with clients to better connect them to the process. For example, a small food products company was searching for the appropriate type and shape of metal box in which to package a new cookie product. Members of the team sent pictures of sample boxes to each other to arrive at a consensus decision.

Sample 1

Sample 2

Final product

* *Whiteboards at meetings.* Photographing the information on a whiteboard not only records data that might normally go

unrecorded, it makes it possible for you to easily distribute an absolutely accurate copy of that information to a work group through e-mail.

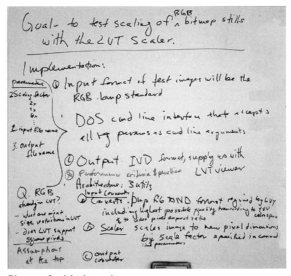

Photo of whiteboard

Solopreneurs: How a Small-Office or Home-Office (SOHO) Business Grows by *Going Visual*

One of the primary underlying concepts of this book is that the democratization of technology—through the Internet and easy-to-use, inexpensive digital cameras and camera phones—opens the doors to *Going Visual* to virtually any businessperson. Sally Carrocino is an independent sales representative offering home and garden accessories of seven manufacturers to clients such as medium- to high-end gift stores, decorators, furniture stores, and garden centers. Carrocino is an example of a *solopreneur* who, with no computer or photography background and by adopting a personal Visual Communication strategy, has, in her words, "totally changed my business, totally revolutionized it."

Like any successful entrepreneur, Carrocino constantly examines her business processes, searching for new opportunities, new ways to be more productive and competitive. She is always on the lookout for techniques that can improve her core skill—communicating—and give her business a boost. In doing so, Carrocino has focused on an irrefutable lesson that 25 years of sales experience has taught her: Words don't sell products—pictures do.

Her five-step process began with a lightbulb moment, when she realized that *Going Visual* could help her overcome major obstacles to growing her business.

Carrocino did not even own a computer until she had her lightbulb moment and realized that *Going Visual* would instantly change the way she communicated with her clients. She remembers: "I had avoided getting a computer; I really didn't think there was a reason for me to have one. I kept my orders in my file and I liked having paper, and so I really didn't see it. Then one day at an industry show, I was working with the owner of a store, and he was taking digital pictures of the products. I asked him what he was

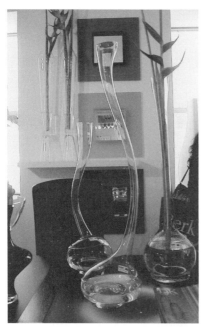 

Samples of Carrocino's product pictures

going to do with the pictures, and he said that at night he down-
loads them and e-mails them to his buyer. The next morning, the
buyer goes into the office, sees the pictures, calls him up and tells
him what to buy. I thought, Oh my god! That's when I decided
that I needed a digital camera. I could relate it to my business
because I was frustrated that many of my manufacturers would
introduce new products at a trade show, but wouldn't provide the
reps with pictures of those products. I'd have to wait and wait until
the catalogs were sent out. For example, as of February 20, I still
hadn't received pictures of products I saw at a show on January 7.
That's a six-week gap! My customers want to see new products
right away, and I don't want them to go and see those products for
themselves at a show where I don't get paid for writing their order.
If I hadn't taken my own pictures, I would not have been able to

sell any of these new products. Every aspect of this speaks to my bottom line."

Carrocino knew that she could not make a sale by describing her products in words—she absolutely needed pictures to show her 150 clients the seven product lines she represents. Although hers is a business that traditionally uses pictures, those pictures were supplied by the manufacturers, so accessing them was out of her control, which impacted an important component of her business process: her selling cycle. Carrocino found herself "dead in the water," she said, unable to sell for weeks at a time. She was a passive user of images who was about to take control and become an active image communicator.

STEP 1. SURVEY

Do an inventory of internal and external corporate communications for instances of written or verbal information that might be significantly improved if replaced or augmented by images.

The survey consisted of reviewing her product lines and determining which of her manufacturers created a significant gap between the time she viewed new products at the trade show and the moment when they provided her with the materials she needed (in the form of catalogs or product sheets) to start her sales process. Carrocino was determined to take control and significantly accelerate the sales process by taking and instantly distributing her own pictures of the new products. She identified her Community of Interest as the seven manufacturers whose lines she represented and the 150 clients to whom she sold those products. She became actively involved in producing images of her manufacturers' products (hence the two-way arrow in the following graphic) and distributed the pictures to all of her clients.

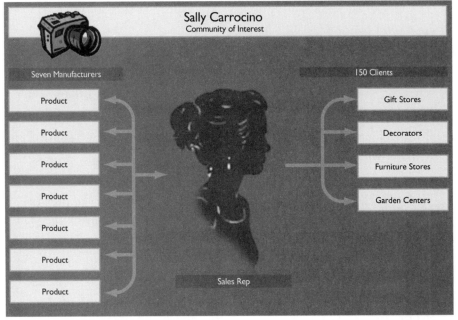

Sally Carrocino's Community of Interest

Personal Business Lifestyle Choice

Sally Carrocino also had an important personal business lifestyle issue that many sales reps can surely relate to. She was tired of lugging a vanful of product samples from customer to customer. By making images an integral part of her personal sales technique, she hoped to communicate the value of her products without having to physically present them to each client. She describes her thoughts at that time: "I started my business with silk flowers, and I had tons and tons of samples and had to drive a van to hold them all. I decided to change my business and sell more lines that I could show in a book of pictures so I did not have to carry a bunch of samples. That's one of the biggest advantages of the digital camera for me, that I can take all of these pictures and not have people say, 'Well, can I see it? I'll wait and see it at a show.' I wanted to do something where they wouldn't be able to say that anymore." *Going Visual* has freed Sally from the van forever.

STEP 2. IMPLEMENT

Equip the appropriate senders and recipients of communications who are Going Visual *with the necessary imaging technology, and train them to use it effectively.*

Although Carrocino is not at all a technology person, it turns out that in her field she is an early adopter, a trailblazer, in using digital photography. She recalls: "I bought my computer because I knew what I was going to be able to do with it and the digital camera. When I got it home, I didn't know how to turn it on—I was afraid to turn it on! I got the computer on the first of March, and I got the digital camera on the first of August. I wanted to wait a little bit to get comfortable on the computer, so I planned a little bit of a learning progression instead of having to take on everything all at once. I also bought a scanner and a printer. Now I make hundreds of prints a month. I have created these books, of about 200 pages each, which hold a combination of my pictures and the manufacturers' catalog pages."

Carrocino's books of photos

A typical page in her book

Learning Curve

Carrocino is the typical nontechie consumer, overwhelmed by the seemingly endless choices of digital cameras in the marketplace. "I was going to a big show in New York," she said, "and the weekend before, I went out and looked at cameras. I didn't know what to buy. I even called a radio computer talk show and told him what I did, that I was a rep and I wanted a camera to take these kinds of pictures, and they gave me a lot of information, but it didn't really narrow it down for me. That Monday, a good friend of mine called and told me that he had heard the program and recognized my voice, and he said, 'Sally, come over and I'll show you what camera to buy.' He showed me his camera's features, which matched my needs, so on his recommendation, I went out and bought it. I hate to read instructions, but on the airplane, flying to New York, I read through them and set the different 'things' to what I thought they should be, and that was it! I got off the plane, went to the show and started to shoot. The settings worked so well I'm still using them. Downloading the pictures was very easy—just one cord from the camera to the computer and push the button."

Return on Investment

Carrocino wasted no time putting her pictures to work. "When I got back from the show, I downloaded and printed the pictures. The following day I had appointments and was able to start selling the new products right away. Just out of curiosity, I kept a running total of the sales that I made directly due to my own pictures. Within four days the commission from those items had paid for my camera. And those are things that I wouldn't have been able to sell for a minimum of six to eight weeks without my pictures."

> In my business, you're trying to get through all these
> different barriers with people. They can think of a lot of

reasons not to buy something. That's why I got my
camera—to not give them those excuses.

—Sally Carrocino

Carrocino also found that once her clients were aware that she could
communicate directly with them through images, they tapped that
power to increase the scope of their orders. By taking control of the
visual information she was creating, she found herself making important decisions about how best to present her products. Instead of communicating generic, prepackaged information, an image-active person
can customize any presentation to speak directly to the targeted clients.
Carrocino: "My clients were so excited when I came back from the
show and was able to show them new product immediately. Another
advantage of the pictures I take is that a couple of the lines do really
fabulous display work with the product, and I capture a lot of that in
my pictures. So besides just showing the client the new product, I'm
showing them great ways to use it. I either e-mail the pictures to them,
or, because a lot of my customers aren't computer-savvy yet—they're a
little bit slow getting started—I make prints and send them. That has
been a huge help in building long-lasting relationships, because now
they are really depending on me for a lot of different things."

She described a specific example of a sale expanded by her use of
images: "I just had a customer who had never bought this one line
before, and she liked a number of different things in a display. The
sales challenge was that she didn't think she would remember what
she wanted to order because she was not buying just one item, she
wanted to buy this whole look. I simply told her I'd take a picture of
that display and send it to her, and that immediately made her feel
really comfortable about ordering everything. In my business, you're
trying to get through all these different barriers with people. They
can think of a lot of reasons not to buy something. That's why I got
my camera—to not give them those excuses."

Sample of a line with a "look"

Carrocino's communication goal is so well defined—to give her clients the best possible visual information about the products she's representing—that she can focus on how to use the modest digital tools at her disposal to get the maximum effect.

STEP 3. ARCHIVE

Create a resource that provides access, retrieval, and storage of the images.

Her archiving strategy evolved from necessity. When she first started taking pictures, she didn't consider that she would quickly have hundreds of images from seven different manufacturers. She used the program that came with her camera to create a simple but effective archive. She recalls her challenge: "All of a sudden I had a ton of pictures from several different lines, different manufacturers. Hundreds of pictures, all lumped together in this folder, and I wanted to be able to sort them by manufacturer. I made a file for every one of my manufacturers and transferred the appropriate pictures into those individual files so that when I need to find them I can do it very easily." Carrocino doesn't have an extensive keyword system because she's more comfortable reviewing her pictures visually. As she puts it, "The most pictures I have in any manufacturer file is 100, and I can view the thumbnails very easily and find what I'm looking for. So naming the files hasn't really been an issue for me."

Carrocino regularly refreshes her archive because the images' sales value lasts no longer than one selling season. She describes her process: "As a product is discontinued, I delete it. I don't need it in my file anymore because it is not available, so it's no longer important to me. At the end of a season—and my seasons run from January through June and July through December—I'll delete most of my pictures and start over fresh, because my customers have already seen them, and one of the things they enjoy is seeing new displays and new pictures."

The simple archiving needs are the result of three factors:

1. She uses her images for only one purpose—selling. Therefore, when an item drops out of her catalog, the useful life of the image that represents it has ended.

2. Since most items last no more than one season, the useful life of the images is very short—only a matter of months.

3. The scale of Carrocino's business is such that the total number of items she has in her archive at any one time is quite small— a few hundred—and therefore does not require a sophisticated indexing and retrieval process.

Companies that operate on a larger scale can put their visual records to multiple uses, some of which unfold over time. Therefore, when they describe their Visual Communication strategies, archiving and retrieval have a much more central role and require greater investments of ingenuity and resources. We present an in-depth look at an extensive image archive in Chapter 6.

STEP 4. TRACK AND EVALUATE

Observe and analyze the effectiveness of the Visual Communication strategy in terms of increased knowledge-worker productivity, better and faster decision making, the promotion of customer loyalty, and the enhancement of overall values and mission of the organization.

For a sales rep like Sally Carrocino, measuring the value of her Visual Communication strategy was very straightforward. As she stated earlier, "Every aspect of this speaks to my bottom line." She reviewed how *Going Visual* has fundamentally improved her business in light of the four essential requirements:

1. *Increasing knowledge-worker productivity.* In this case, Carrocino targeted her own productivity by becoming an image-active entrepreneur and communicating to her clients more efficiently and effectively than she'd ever done before. In terms of her own productivity, the technology was an accelerator well worth its cost. "The digital camera has just been so easy," she said, "because you can take a picture and you can see it right away. You don't have that downtime of taking it to the store and getting it developed. What I spend the most money on is ink and paper, but I don't mind because it's part of my business expense, and what I spend on it I get back tenfold."

2. *Enhancing decision-making support.* By using her own images, Carrocino moved her clients to buy more products in shorter sales cycles. "I'm selling more products, faster, to my customers, and they're getting the product faster, and then they're reordering faster. My sales have increased over 30 percent since I got the digital camera. Another thing that inspired me to use a digital camera was that some of the companies I work with print black-and-white catalogs, which don't really show all the different finishes they offer. Going to the show and taking color pictures has made a big difference in being able to show clients the different displays. I put my color picture alongside the black-and-white picture from the catalog. There's nothing worse than visiting customers and hearing them say, 'I can't tell what this looks like.' My pictures have solved that problem. I relate everything to pictures."

3. *Promoting loyalty in both customers and suppliers.* With image-centric, value-added services other reps do not offer, Carrocino stays ahead of her competition. *Going Visual* has differentiated Carrocino from her competition. She described the unique link she has forged: "My customers always say, 'Other reps don't bring me these great pictures,' and they always want to see more. Once we're through looking at my book of lines, they'll say 'What else have you got?' They are so enthusiastic about me and my products."

She continued: "I believe I have a competitive edge with my digital camera, because in my industry, the other reps aren't doing it. My manufacturers are thrilled with what I do. When they see that I'm taking this initiative and doing more for their lines, it puts me in a much better light. We talk about it and we're amazed that more reps aren't doing it. In our industry, it's just been a little bit slow starting. They're excited when I bring out my camera and start taking pictures. It's been a really good asset for me in building rapport with my manufacturers, I've become more embedded with my manufacturers, which is really important. They like the fact that I'm inventive and go the extra mile."

4. *Enhancing the overall values and mission of the organization.* In this case, Carrocino had personal business lifestyle goals, which she achieved by *Going Visual.* "On a personal level, I also wanted to get out of the van, and now I have a cool car. I carry hardly any samples. I have just a few, and 9 times out of 10, I don't even need to bring them in because my pictures are enough. Even when I bring in the samples for color or texture or quality, people always go back to the pictures because they can see the whole thing, as opposed to all of these individual pieces. They want to see one actual piece and feel it, but then they always go back to the pictures."

Carrocino's new business lifestyle

STEP 5. REASSESS AND EDUCATE

Having identified the areas of greatest gains, invest in them further to maximize benefits to the organization. Learn about the application of emerging visual technologies and evaluate how those technologies could solve additional business problems.

Sally Carrocino has come a long way from the days when she ran her business with paper files and no camera. All the positive growth of her business is linked to *Going Visual*. She reflected on what she's learned: "I really didn't think that I was a good candidate for a computer, and then, with the digital camera, I realized that I had to have a computer. I use it for so many things. I was so naive when I didn't think it was applicable in my business, because it is; and not just my business, it's applicable in my daily life." Carrocino has discovered that the lines that used to divide personal and business technologies are disappearing. The same computer that solopreneurs use for business communication also links them to family and friends. The same digital camera used for taking pictures of products also records kids, pets, and birthday parties. The universal language of images knows no bounds.

Although Sally Carrocino was able to start selling products immediately after learning how to use the camera, she quickly realized that once she had taken the leap to producing her own pictures, other possibilities opened up. Her increased sales had already proven that a picture is worth a thousand words; now she wanted to add text to those pictures to give them even more value and further shorten the decision-making process. She described how she approached this challenge in her typically intuitive way: "As I went along, I realized that there were other things that I wanted to be able to do with my pictures. One of those things was to insert text, because I wanted to put style numbers and prices on the photos. I was printing using the program that came with the camera, and I thought, 'There's got to be a way to add text to these pictures.' So I just played. A friend encouraged me by saying, 'Just play with it, just click all the buttons, and you can't screw anything up 'cause it'll always come on and say, 'So you want to delete this?' I was clicking, clicking, and then I found the 'insert text' button, and I started using it; then it took me a while to figure out how to keep it on the page, and finally it stayed there. That changed everything, and I went back to my pictures and added text."

As simple as that description sounds, adding text allowed Carrocino to begin to produce simple but effective catalogs. One of those early catalogs provided her with a potent competitive weapon.

Carrocino's typical catalog page

Making the First Catalog

"I got a line once, a really good [product] line that did not have a catalog," Carrocino said. "Before I got the line, when I was pursuing them [the manufacturers], I took a ton of pictures of their booth.

When I came home, I created a print catalog of their products. My catalog turned out to be really valuable, because when they called me up and they said, 'You've got the line,' I was able to go out and sell it the very next day. If I had waited for them to send me pictures, it would have been months, and I don't have the patience for that! I wanted to fax them an order the next day, and I did! Soon they were calling me, asking, 'How are you writing all these orders?' The next show I went to, because I was so proud of it, I brought my catalog, and they were blown away."

Camera-Phone Future

Looking ahead to the next stage of her Visual Communication strategy, Sally Carrocino thought that a camera phone would be useful for creating a visual diary, a way to record how her day was spent. "The camera phone would be more for fun and spontaneity," she said. "I would use the camera phone if I was out at a customer and had to take a picture of a problem, or if I liked a customer's display. That's come up several times, where I've kicked myself because I didn't have my camera. I really should keep it in my car all the time, and that's where a camera phone would be important, because I always have my phone with me. Sometimes I'll go into a store and they'll have done something really neat, and I'd like to be able to put it in my book to show other customers. Or, if there's a line that I like and I want to find the manufacturer, it could work for me as a visual notepad." Carrocino's thoughts on carrying a camera phone to grab shots when she doesn't have her digital camera underscores the blending of personal and business lifestyles we described earlier.

When we spoke to Jeff Hallock, vice president of product marketing and strategy for Sprint, he saw this blend as a driving force in the rapidly growing adoption of camera phones. Said Hallock: "I really think there are two things that are coming together here. First, the mobile phone has become the single device that you're going to carry other than the keys in your pocket. It's typically always with people. It used to be that if I left the house in the morning and forgot my wallet, I would go back and get it. These days, people who leave their mobile phone at home are certainly going to turn around and go get it, because it's become that integral to their life. If I have a phone with a camera in it, I am going to communicate more. I use a single phone for both business and consumer purposes, and I have an e-mail account that I might use for both business and consumer purposes. What we've found is, customers will take pictures of things that they may never have thought about taking a picture of before, because they're thinking of it from the perspective of a communication that's instant, on the spot. So there are more pictures being taken since the advent of mobile phones than previously with the camera business only."

In Chapter 5, we spotlight a retail sales and manufacturing organization that is using camera phones to instantly communicate visual information around the world.

There is more in Carrocino's future than even she recognizes today. The *Going Visual* strategy that has so enhanced her success uses only some of the tools available to her industry. She has yet to fully explore the huge benefits of the Internet and the capacity to exchange information instantly with her customers and suppliers through computers and camera phones.

Sally Carrocino sums up the value of *Going Visual* this way: "It's totally changed my business. Totally revolutionized it. Last year was the best year I've ever had, and a lot of it has to do with what I've put together in these books. And the thing is, it's fun! I really love it. I love playing, because there's a part of me, a creative sense, that I get to release. It all comes back to the digital camera and my computer. I know that for sure."

PRACTICAL EXERCISE

Try creating photo images for the following purposes:

- *Safety planning for your facilities.* A tour of your facility done in still images or video can uncover problems and help the staff visualize emergency procedures. These images can be distributed or posted throughout the organization.

- *Training.* Take a series of snapshots or a short video that can be used to capture how to perform a task.

Visual Literacy

With images becoming an essential component of everyday business communications, success in the workplace will require a new skill, which we call *visual literacy*—the ability to read images intelligently and to use images articulately to express oneself. Just as today a large part of the impression we create is based on how well we use language, whether speaking or writing, how well we use images will become a key element of how we are perceived.

Using images to convey the specialized information that businesses use to make decisions is different from the art of photography, which emphasizes the aesthetic value of images. The value of an image as decision support is measured by how effectively that image communicates the specific information the sender intends. If, for example, a particular device, in this case a gauge on a truck, has to

(Continued)

(Continued)

be installed in a precise location, the image must convey that message to the viewer.

Truck gauge location

From a visual literacy aspect, the creator of the image must capture the visual information in a manner that is clear, concise, and involves as little ambiguity as possible to the eye of the viewer—remembering that the viewer is not familiar with the visual information to begin with. The viewer must be provided with the context within which to interpret the meaning of the information captured in the image. This context may be in the form of text or voice metadata, or as a series of photographs showing other views of the scene being captured. In this case, the gauge is installed in the truck shown.

Dan Steinhardt, marketing manager of Epson America, posed the visual literacy question this way, "Anyone can take a picture, but we must find ways to help people who are not visual communicators by training them how to use imaging devices so that they can communicate their views effectively. How can we help educate people who are never going to be professional photographers create images that are visually interesting and that effectively communicate information?"

One succinct answer to that question came from educator and photographer Katrin Eismann who observed, "Communicating visually is all about showing relationships. If you are a businessperson sent by your company to look at leasing an office, and you are using images to show your colleagues your opinion, what you have to convey is: 'This is my point of view on this space, this is why I

(Continued)

(Continued)

feel that I can (or can't) work here.' You want to show your relationship to that office, and that office's relationship to its environment. For example, you might take a photograph outside the door to show what the office looks like as you are approaching it, because if you are renting an office you want to know what kind of an impression people are going to have when they come and visit you. And you should take a picture of the view outside, because that's a relationship: The image shows that 'this office overlooks the valley.' Most people walking into an office environment are going to take pictures of the first thing that grabs their attention, and those pictures are going to look like typical real estate pictures, because that's something we're all familiar with, so we try to conform to it. What a visually literate person does instead is take pictures that show their relationship to the environment, and the relationships that exist within the environment."

Whether the pictures are of a retail environment, a construction site, a piece of equipment, or a billboard, showing context and relationships are key rules for effectively communicating visually.

CHAPTER 5

Imaging Every Day and Everywhere: How a Midsized Business Wins by Going from Text to Image

ally Carrocino's experience makes the case for *Going Visual* from the point of view of an individual entrepreneur—in her case, a sales rep who discovered the power of creating images and uses them to improve her results through better communication. To see how images are being used to dramatic effect by those who receive them, those who are being communicated to visually, we turn to Michelle Kline, senior vice president of merchandising for a chain of stores in Carrocino's market of medium- to high-end gift stores, furniture stores, and garden centers. Kline said her company has been "catapulted" by *Going Visual,* particularly "in terms of being able to get product to market more quickly and communicating with her agents worldwide." Kline's company is sensitive to the competitive environment in which it operates and has requested that we identify it with a pseudonym; in this chapter, it will be identified as "HomeGo."

Kline is responsible for running the merchandising department, where she's involved in the development, design, manufacturing, and marketing of the company's many products. She is also responsible for making sure that each product is appropriately displayed in its catalog, in its stores, and on its web site.

In this case, we focus on communications that are not traditionally of a visual nature. HomeGo does use images to sell products, but the images of interest to us are those used to manage what happens *behind* the scenes, specifically the interaction between the store and its warehouse locations, merchandising, product research, design, manufacturing, and quality control. These are areas where the new power of images transforms the enterprise. The images Kline receives come from inside her organization, sent, for instance, by district store managers and staff buyers and by an eclectic mix of sources around the world, including independent sales agents, product manufacturers, and designers.

HomeGo's retail stores are all located in the United States, but the company researches, purchases, and manufactures its goods all over the world. From identifying a rare species of plant found in Paris to documenting a uniquely beautiful lamp detail seen in Italy, from doing quality control on a product manufactured in Europe to monitoring in-store displays in Chicago, images have become Kline's second language. The global marketplace is a treasure trove of innovative products and ideas that can't be adequately described in words. Images have become the way to share that knowledge. When someone is doing something innovative anywhere in the world, images empower Kline to see that innovation, make a judgment, and instantly distribute the visual information to the appropriate members in her Community of Interest.

Kline's Community of Interest includes independent buying agents all over the world, product designers, manufacturers, district-store sales managers, an internal group of management decision makers, and the company's marketing, sales, and customer relations departments. HomeGo's *Going Visual* strategy evolved very quickly.

STEPS 1, 2, AND 3. SURVEY, IMPLEMENT, ARCHIVE

HomeGo's use of visual communication began only nine months before our conversation, in a casual, tactical way, when its CEO bought a camera phone and for the first time had an image-capturing device with him at all times. Kline described how use of the camera phone as a visual notepad became the impetus for the company to embrace *Going Visual* as an important strategic business tool: "He started using it on business trips, taking pictures of products we might be interested in, plants, and whatnot. Then he started going to the stores and taking pictures of our displays so that we could look at them as a management team and decide whether they

Store display

were right or wrong. These displays are the driving force behind our sales, and if they are not right, the sales suffer. The in-store pictures he took were so effective in helping us make decisions relating to point-of-purchase sales that we came to the realization that we should have the local district managers take pictures and send them to us so we can look at them regularly and monitor the stores."

The CEO's successful use of images provided a sampling of the kind of valuable information that can be easily gathered visually—pictures of in-store displays and potential products. That ad hoc *survey* served as an effective step 1 for the company to target two sets of employees—district managers and merchandise-buying teams—which in turn provided the platform to launch step 2, to *implement* an in-house *Going Visual* strategy. Kline explained: "We sent digital cameras to our district managers, who take pictures of their in-store displays and also document anything at their location that might be broken and need repair." The company quickly realized that it would be beneficial to receive images from its buyers and manufacturers across the world. It bought an international camera phone for its in-house buying team, and was pleasantly surprised to discover that its European and Asian independent agents had already gone visual and bought their own camera phones.

As the number of images coming in from the stores grew, the company proceeded rapidly to step 3, establishing a suitable but simple *archive* that focused on images relating to the stores. The managers send the images to the management team, and they are stored in a shared file that is organized by store, by date, and by issue. Each district manager is responsible for organizing and submitting images for the weekly review. This system allows all the pictures of the product displays in the stores on a particular date to be reviewed by management for quality, consistency, and placement. It also enables management to view all the images involving the issue of damaged goods or facilities maintenance.

Before describing how the company dealt with steps 4 and 5, we examine the multitude of benefits it reaped in various areas of the organization by *Going Visual.*

Store and Warehouse Management

At the store and warehouse level, Kline noted that "when you bring the goods into the country, frequently they get broken on the way, and when the product arrives at the store it's damaged. I get an e-mail with pictures of the damaged product from a manager saying that 'this product is cracked, or this hinge is wrong, or the quality of this wood is substandard.' Not only am I getting immediate information, I'm also getting tools that I can use to act immediately—

images I can pass on to the manufacturer for reference. This happens at our warehouse, our stores; it happens all the way along the line. We also receive pictures of damaged products from customers, and because we can see and identify their problem, there are fewer disputes during our resolution discussions."

Damaged furniture sample

Kline said, "Often we'll print these images so we can all share them at our meetings. Ultimately, the goal is that during our weekly calls with these district managers we can look at the images—either as prints or on a big screen in our conference room—while we're talking to them so we are all referencing exactly the same information."

The company quickly realized an additional, and very significant, cost saving benefit as a result of these visual reports of in-store conditions. "Using images helps in managing our expenses," Kline said. "I used to spend a lot of my time traveling to individual stores to see the layouts. Now I can do most of that by looking at the pictures in my office."

Merchandising

Just as Sally Carrocino is out in the field, visiting trade shows and customer sites, collecting images of new products and merchandising ideas and sending them to her clients, Michelle Kline has agents all around the world using digital cameras and camera phones as visual notepads, harvesting product and design ideas, and sending those pictures to her. Kline explained: "We gave our buying teams digital cameras to take on their trips, with instructions to photograph everything they see so that we know exactly what we're talking about in reference to a price or a quote. In this industry you really want to see the product; you want to visualize it to have some refer-

Plant identification photo

ence to that product when you're talking about it with vendors. The small size of the camera really made this possible, the ease of carrying it with you and popping it out and having these little disks filled with pictures that document your trip. For example, they go to the plant show, where they see all the new plant species developed for the international market. You can't really ship these plants around for viewing because they are highly regulated. Our buyer might go to a booth and find 50 kinds of lavender. You'd have to be an expert in order to understand the difference between one kind of lavender and another. Many times in our travels we see plants that we can't identify. With a camera, however, you get to take something back with you besides the Latin botanical name so that we can consult reference materials and experts within our team and make fully informed decisions. Having pictures humanizes the process."

Product Resourcing and Design

Kline has found that the independent agents she works with worldwide are much more advanced than their American counterparts in their commitment to *Going Visual*. "I don't think I know a single agent in Europe or Asia who doesn't have a camera phone," she said. "It's clearly something that they believe is crucial to doing business. So far this year, I've traveled to many continents, and in every single case the agents had a digital camera in their phone. One agent travels up and down the countryside, where all the factories are outside the big cities. Because she's in her car so much and she can't e-mail from there, she takes the photographs, sends them from the camera phone to her office, then calls her assistant and tells her what to write about each photo in the e-mail. This allows her to send the visual information and the documentation to us while she herself is on the move spotting new opportunities rather than stuck in the office doing the low-value part of the communication process."

Kline described how these sharp-eyed agents are using pictures to communicate vast amounts of information that simply couldn't effectively be put into words alone. "Our independent agents around the world are looking for product for us. They might be walking down the street in Moscow, they might be at the New York Exhibit, and they're taking photographs. Our agent in China recently sent us numerous pictures of potential products—an amount of information that would have been almost impossible to communicate through language—to use as inspiration for products we would design."

She continued, "Our designers are focused on creating designs for manufacturing; we don't invest in maintaining a staff of artists to invent new ideas. Receiving large numbers of pictures that give us product ideas, like our Chinese agent sent, allows us to give our designers a visual reference point to base a design on. We can say to them, 'This one element over here, this curlicue, is perfect. Let's make it in wrought iron, or let's make it in aluminum.' We most frequently print the images and lay the pictures out side by side so that we can see them all. That's one thing computer screens are not so good at—you've got a whole string of digital pictures and you can't see them all at once, so you've got to click back and forth to remember what you saw. Prints work really well for us in this part of the process. We then combine the images with written documentation that tells the designer how to utilize the details, and that's extremely useful."

Kline has found that even designers working in very traditional ways have found simple but empowering ways to go visual. "A fascinating thing that's happened is that designers are sending us drawings and renderings as digital pictures. We'll decide we want to build a trellis with some design elements we've seen, and a designer working at home will sketch it, then shoot a picture of the sketch with his camera phone and send it to us. Suddenly, you've got a very rudimentary sort of old-world activity, *sketching*, which through the use of digital photography allows us to expedite the creative decision-making process. Here's a dramatic example. I received an e-mail from one of our agents that said, 'Your buyer is out of the country. Please look at these photographs of my sketches and give me input.' I printed his pictures out and then systematically went through them and gave him input so that he could then create a few samples, which he's going to bring with him when he's here next week. We gave him the project no more than three weeks ago. For us to have a sample by next week is shocking."

Camera phone picture of a design drawing

This blending of traditional techniques with modern visual communication is simplifying and streamlining the decision-making process and lowering the overhead at the point of communication to a negligible amount. The designer simply needs a camera phone, a piece of paper, and a pen to quickly have an idea evaluated. That makes for a big decrease in the traditional cost structure, which in terms of both time and materials has direct benefits to the bottom line.

Manufacturing and Quality Control

Once the design has been sent to the manufacturer, the production and approval process begins. This is an area where time to market is a critical bottom-line issue. Kline explained how *Going Visual* saves time and money. "Because of the necessity to bring product to market quickly, I was literally sending product samples all over the world by FedEx, and that gets expensive. Now we take pictures and send them, and then we can decide whether we want to spend the money to FedEx something based on our impression from a photograph. That's

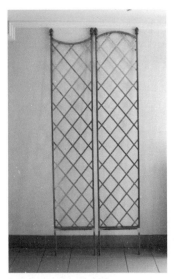

become incredibly valuable. Decision making can be so much quicker than if you're shipping this stuff back and forth. It used to be that the manufacturer would make a sample and we'd FedEx it over here, and then we say, 'You've got the wrong hinges on there.' By using pictures, we save shipping costs, and time—which is critical."

Every single day, I get images that represent what used to be a lot of words.

Product-approval picture   **—Michelle Kline**

The power of pictures mated to the speed of the Internet has made the visual conversation a constant part of Kline's business life. She reflected: "I get pictures all the time, every day—it's now become the way of doing business. There are all these different pieces of the puzzle; from reps for companies and agents who represent manufacturers to designers, everyone is using digital images to communicate information quickly. When manufacturers make a prototype of a sample product, they will send images for approval. This morning, for example, I got a bunch of photographs of a product that I'm having made, and it has scratches on it. The agent sent a message along, saying, 'Look at these digital images that I took in my office. I'm not satisfied with what's happening with this product. I want to know if you agree.' So before they incur the expense of shipping me the sample, which has to go through a specific type of testing, they send me photographs. Every single day, I get images that represent what used to be a lot of words. Instead of sending me a lot of words that say, 'This is wrong and that's wrong,' they are using the digital images to say, 'I have a problem.' " The visual conversation is the solution.

The communication process Kline describes is an excellent example of the dynamic flow of images through the Community of Interest. Images are sent to the company from agents around the world, who identify design details in objects they are viewing. Kline's product merchandising team then evaluates those images, and the interesting elements are collected and assembled in a document, which is then sent to independent designers who work their magic and, in turn, send images of their work back to the team. The team, which makes its production decisions based on the images, might require changes, perhaps sending the designer images of more details to be added or removed. The team then sends the designs to the manufacturer, who builds a prototype, which is photographed, and those images are sent to the team for approval. At every step in the process,

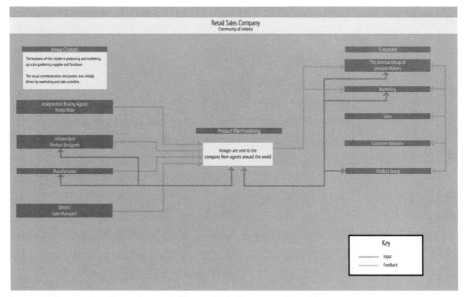

Image-information flow through HomeGo's Community of Interest

images have become the key instrument of communication, and being image-enabled is essential to the community's success.

STEP 4. TRACK AND EVALUATE

In only nine months, the elements of *Going Visual* have imbedded themselves throughout this organization, and HomeGo's management has acknowledged this contribution to the company's competitive edge by requesting that we keep its name anonymous. Our four key criteria for success have been met:

1. *Increasing knowledge-worker productivity.* Many members of this diverse Community of Interest have benefited by using images instead of or in addition to words to communicate—often from locations around the world—visually rich, specific information about new products, designs, and in-store issues.

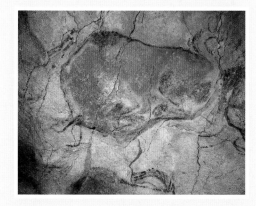

Altamira cave
painting
(text page 20)

Hyder
housing site
(text page 59)

Typical Hyder
landscaping example
(text page 63)

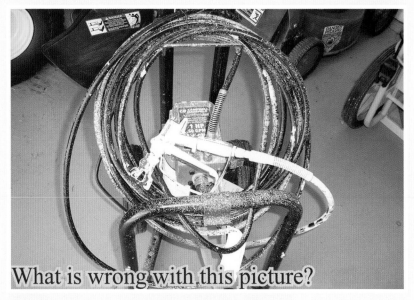

Hyder maintenance training photo (text page 78)

Sally Carrocino
product group photo
(text page 88)

Sally Carrocino product group photo (text page 91)

Sally Carrocino product group photo (text page 94)

Truck gauge maintenance photo (text page 104)

Truck maintenance photo (text page 105 and 151)

HomeGo store
display
(text page 111)

HomeGo new plant
product example
(text page 114)

Clear Channel billboard example (text page 131)

MIT Media Lab telepresence screen (text page 172)

Temperate forest natural ecosystem example (text page 185)

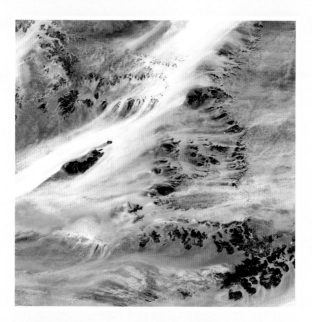

LandSat satellite photo (text page 199)

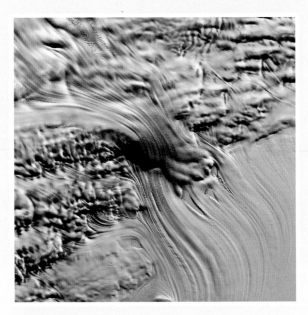

LandSat satellite photo (text page 199)

Going Visual, whether by using camera phones or digital cameras, has greatly accelerated not only the speed at which they can send information to the enterprise, but also the accuracy of the communication. The use of images has greatly decreased the need for executives to travel to store locations and has reduced the cost and time involved in shipping product prototypes to the company for evaluation.

2. *Enhancing decision-making support.* Images have now become indispensable to, in Michelle Kline's words, "making fully informed decisions." Whether assessing the quality of a new product as part of the manufacturing process, choosing a design detail as part of product development, judging the effectiveness of an in-store display for merchandising and sales purposes, or evaluating damaged products for customer service, *Going Visual* has profoundly improved the decision-making process.

3. *Promoting customer loyalty.* By using images to better manage the quality of the in-store displays, monitor damaged goods before they go on sale, and deal with customers via customer service, the company is meeting and exceeding the expectations of its clients.

4. *Enhancing the overall values and mission of the organization.* Because images now play a key role in improving the bedrock functions of the organization, their use enhances the quality of the company's products and the interaction between its employees, agents, suppliers, customers, and manufacturers. *Going Visual* has catapulted the company to a secure and competitive position in the international marketplace.

Clearly, this retail sales company has profited in significant ways from a modest investment in a handful of digital cameras and camera phones and its understanding of the importance of interacting with the quickly emerging, visually enabled world.

STEP 5. REASSESS AND EDUCATE

Having identified the areas of greatest gains, invest in them further to maximize benefits to the organization. Learn about the application of emerging visual technologies, and evaluate how those technologies could solve additional business problems.

A future *Going Visual* innovation the company is exploring is the addition of videoconferencing capabilities. At present, HomeGo uses large-screen monitors in its conference room to review images and presentations, but hasn't added full videoconferencing. Kline described how some of the company's international suppliers have demonstrated the value of videoconferencing: "Some of our bigger agents, in cities like Hong Kong, have put in rooms that have video-conferencing, and that's expediting things. They can sit in a room and show us a problem. We don't happen to have that yet, but depending on the cost, I could see us adding it."

In Chapter 7, we give a detailed account of the value of video-conferencing.

PRACTICAL EXERCISE

Virtually any business with people who report from the field can benefit from *Going Visual*. In a sales scenario, a distributor of a retail product wants to know that the product has reached the store and is being displayed in exactly the manner called for under contract. Let's take a product we're all familiar with, books in a bookstore, as an example. The book business has a diverse Community of Interest focused on the retail sales environment. Members of the community include publishers, authors, agents, publicists, the literary press, distributors, printers, bookstore owners, local store managers, field sales reps, and advertising agencies. If a sales campaign is linked to an in-store marketing effort, it could be very valuable for the distributor's field sales reps to carry digital cameras in order to visually record and communicate the actual store-by-store implementation of the campaign. Photographs would reassure those in the community that the proper displays are in the stores at the time and in the place they were contracted for—or would alert them that they are not. The photos that follow would tell everyone in the Community of Interest whether this particular location is doing its job—as well as providing some interesting information that would never appear in a written report. In this case, the publisher's book display was positioned next to a very popular Beatles music release.

In-store sales display—Glendale, California, December 20, 2003

The following information-rich images tell a valuable story at a glance. One month later, at another store, the book was still being prominently displayed.

In-store display—Highland Park, Illinois, January 21, 2004

Smart Images: Making Images Work Systemically, Over Time, Throughout a Larger Company

O nce you go visual, images begin to flow through the organization and through the broader Community of Interest. One picture leads to another, and in no time hundreds, even thousands, of images are in the system. For these images to stay alive and useful they must "get smart." They must be endowed with the kind of associated information that enables them to be found, organized, analyzed, integrated, transmitted, displayed, viewed, and printed. A smart archive of information must be created. John Meyer, of HP Labs, puts the importance of the archiving at the top of any *Going Visual* strategy: "Most of the future of business communication will be dependent on establishing a visual base of information now. You won't be ready for the future we're describing if you don't build the archives."

The preceding chapters have tracked *Going Visual* strategies from their inception through their deployment and initial reassessment. We thought it would be helpful at this juncture to examine a company that was further down the visual path in order to discuss the challenges that present themselves in managing tens of thousands of new images every month, as well as maintaining a sizable repository of stored images. This chapter focuses on how a large organization, the 3,600-person outdoor advertising division of Clear Channel Communications, puts smart imaging principles into practice. The outdoor division has established an ingenious visual and textual archiving system that services a complex Community of Interest, delivering image-rich information in the form of contracts, reports, presentations, sales and marketing materials, and invoices. It all begins with making each individual image smart by tagging it with very specific information that can be understood and accessed by the entire system.

The World Wide Web is the greatest archive of information in the history of humankind, and it works because in its infancy sophisticated search engines were developed that made it possible for virtually anyone to find a specific piece of information on any far-flung subject. The user-friendliness of modern search engines like Google gives information seekers the confidence to dig into the universe of billions of web pages with a simple query, with the expectation of getting the correct answer, without knowing or caring how the system works. This transparent experience is possible because the search engines analyze a web page's text and cross-reference that information with a search query.

Searching for images is a different kind of challenge, because present image-analysis software is simply not sophisticated enough to scan an image and describe its contents accurately. Colors and shapes can be identified, but a search engine will not find a picture with the specific content of, say, "a billboard advertisement for a Breitling brand wristwatch, placed in Palos Verdes, California, during October, November, and December of this year by Morgan's Jewelers," unless that information has been connected to the image. In order to be found when needed—the criterion for usefulness— this image needs to become smart by having relevant data assigned to it in a way that makes it easily accessible to all members of the Community of Interest.

The Clear Channel case provides a fascinating study of an enterprise in which the uses of images began as a simple record-keeping device for its core profit center—the billboard locations—then proliferated throughout the organization to become an indispensable communication tool for the majority of individuals in every department. Speed and flexibility of information dissemination, plus the accuracy and specificity of that information, were key drivers in this effort. Clients began demanding critical information, such as confirmation that a project was actually completed at a specific location on the contracted date, for which text documents alone were insufficient. Verifiable, image-enhanced documents provided the seeing-is-believing solution. Clear Channel is an excellent example of an enterprise that has adopted image-enhanced communication as a core value.

The roots of Clear Channel Outdoor go back to the Foster & Kleiser Advertising Company, founded in 1901. Foster & Kleiser established most of the standards used by the modern out-of-home-advertising industry. In 1995, the original Foster & Kleiser operation became Eller Media Company, which was acquired by Clear Channel Communications in 1997.

Clear Channel Outdoor, one of the largest outdoor-advertising companies in the world, has 56 offices in the United States, serving 65 countries. Its business is marketing and selling advertising space, creating the displays, and deploying the media, while constructing and maintaining a vast physical infrastructure in the field. The company's clients are advertisers, ranging from mom-and-pop stores to the biggest corporations in the world, and the agencies and media-buying services that represent them. Its outdoor media vary from traditional highway billboards to Times Square Spectacolor video displays, taxi tops, shopping mall displays, mobile truck panels, and bus, train station, and airport advertising. Clear Channel has more than 750,000 advertising surfaces around the world.

Russ Mason, Clear Channel's corporate director of digital services, has been a champion of visual communication for more than 20 years and has led the organization's digital evolution for the past

Traditional billboard

Times Square Spectacolor

Taxi top

Shopping mall display

Mobile panel truck

Bus display

Transit shelter

decade. He opened our conversation on a very high note: "Everything that we envisioned over the last 10 or 12 years has now either come to fruition or is right on the verge of it. We have archived images of all our billboard locations in the United States. We currently capture and input approximately 27,000 new images into the system every month. All these images are digital: The billboard location maps are digital; the supporting text data is digital; and all these pieces come together in databases which make everything online searchable, downloadable, e-mailable, and printable. We use PDF [Portable Document Format] to keep our image-rich documents to file sizes that can travel easily through our network while retaining their original quality for on-screen viewing and printing. The system reaches into so many parts of our business: sales, marketing, accounting, client relations, creative, corporate relations, PR, IT, operations, maintenance, and real estate. We use images everywhere."

Using images everywhere, as Clear Channel does, is possible only when some fundamentally sound image-information preparation has been done. The basic building block is extensive text annotation of every image. This text becomes metadata, which travels with the image wherever it goes on the network and provides tags that can be searched and retrieved for a myriad of uses. Here is a visual presentation of the difference between a smart and not-so-smart image.

Not so smart—an image alone, unsupported by data

ID#157225	2.70 MB	EMCLIB-01-0123.jpg
Keyword / Lexicon		wristwatches watches bands watch rings cameras goods optical necklaces gems earrings jewelry, costume jewelry
long_name		Index / DigitalImageLibrary / Domestic Outdoor / Clothing_and_Accessories / EMCLIB-01-0123.jpg
Time / Location		Day-Field - Palos Verdes, CA
Record ID		1572225
file_name		EMCLIB-01-0123.jpg
file_size		2702440
Description		watch plane
Advertiser		Breitling Morgan's Jewelers
Tag Line		Instruments for Professionals
Date entered		2004-10-25
Date Created		2004-10-25
File type		JPEG
country		US
Embellishments		Illuminated Unit
Display Format		Premiere Panel
Substrate		Computer Vinyl
expiration_date		0000-00-00

Smart! An image and its supporting data

There can be no doubt which image is ready to be used everywhere and which is not. Every word in the preceding display can be plugged into a search to help find this particular image. In this chapter we describe the building of the smart archive from which this information is accessible throughout the organization. We then follow these images through their many uses in the Clear Channel Community of Interest.

STEP 1. SURVEY: THE ROAD TO SMART IMAGING

Because we are picking up the Clear Channel story at an advanced stage, the company had already identified many types of communication that had gone visual, and its survey process was directed at better integrating images into its document information work flow. The more ways the images could be used, the more valuable they became.

Historically, Clear Channel had many different databases: accounting, real estate, contracts, maps, images, and so on. These databases were not integrated into one system. Clear Channel hired an outside consulting firm that audited its information processes and then pulled together a task force of people from all the different parts of the company for a week of brainstorming. The outcome was the creation of an internal, cross-departmental group that was charged with streamlining the company's information work flow to adapt to the changing communication requirements of doing business, which, significantly, included the ever-more ubiquitous use of images. Based on a needs-evaluation study, which looked at things such as how proposals, contracts, and billing documents were generated, the company assigned its in-house programming and engineering group to tie together the information in all the databases.

On the sales, marketing, and accounting fronts, Clear Channel created three systems: Fast Pitch, Market View, and POP, each capable of accessing data company-wide. Each was specifically designed to integrate up-to-the minute text and image information in order to streamline the internal communication within the ClearChannel team and enhance the team's outreach to its clients. Russ Mason describes the three systems and their benefits:

1. *Fast Pitch.* "This is a proposal generator that has really changed the way we do business. The account executive can access this database to pull together and integrate all the elements of a proposal. With Fast Pitch, everything you want to know about that whole contract, including the text descriptions, photographs, and the maps of all the proposed locations, are in one database."

2. *Market View.* "This is a tracking system which starts with the initial proposal and traces the contract all the way through the Proof of Performance document. This gives us a new way to do business nationally by enabling sales managers, general managers, and salespeople nationwide to keep track of who the various offices are calling so that they can coordinate their efforts with a shared visual record of current sales-account activities. Market View is also used to generate case studies that show us the evolution of that business, which tells us what the problem was, what the proposed solution was, how we solved the problem, and what the outcome was."

   This approach is applicable to many businesses with ongoing client relationships. Recalling our Hyder & Company example, a Market View approach would work very well in providing the owner of any site with a vivid, comprehensive visual history of Hyder's management of any given property. From maintenance and construction to tenant relations, the evolution of that business could be quickly assembled and communicated.

3. *Proof of Performance (POP).* "This is a visual record, sent to the client with the invoice, that confirms that the contracted displays have, in fact, been deployed in the correct locations at the correct time. The reason for the POP system is a financial one: If the clients don't see the pictures, they don't pay their bills. With the POP system we can access the contract, and, by inputting the display structure numbers, we can pull up all the appropriate photos. The supporting organization is already in the data, so all we have to do is input the information from the invoice."

This is a crucial use of images that cuts right to the bottom line: timely payment of the invoice. Specific, unambiguous visual information linked directly to contract information is useful in numerous scenarios, such as construction progress photos, property insurance claims, product placement in retail environments (supermarkets, bookstores, department stores), and equipment or fixture installation.

STEP 2. IMPLEMENTING THE ARCHIVE

This is how Clear Channel identifies its image databases.

The Database

The basic components of this system, image-based data, includes photographs of structures, advertising content, installations, equipment, locations, creative images, and maps. These images are tagged with the supporting text

(Continued)

(Continued)

data that makes them "smart." There are three dedicated image databases, which hold a total of more than 800,000 images:

1. *Bulletin Inventory Search (BIS).* Each of Clear Channel's 56 offices has a dedicated server that stores images of all the displays in the area served by that office. These repositories are the main source of images used for billing and site-specific sales, marketing, and operations.

Typical BIS image

2. *Digital Image Library (DIL).* The DIL has images of all types of outdoor displays dating back to the beginning of the company in 1901. The account executive goes to the marketing manager and says, "I need to show a client examples of fashion billboards," and they go to the DIL and search it and pull down these images.

Creative example from DIL

3. *The Exchange.* This database contains licensed, royalty-free images—marketing materials, spec art—a whole list of elements that creative artists in the company can use to generate advertisements for clients or marketing material for the company.

Creating the Lexicon

With the document work-flow systems in place, Clear Channel turned its attention to the construction of its smart-image databases. Since text is used to help make images smart, it is essential that the vocabulary used be standardized company-wide. Therefore, one of the critical components of Clear Channel's strategy was the development of a corporate lexicon, a dictionary of words used to describe its many products and client categories. Because he understood how important the creation of this lexicon would be to the overall success of the *Going Visual* strategy, Mason hired an information science consultant, Linda Rudell-Betts, to coordinate the process. "To begin," says Mason, "we had to come up with the 16 main categories that describe our business, and then go much deeper into concepts like display categories in order to organize the images so they could be easily searched."

The Importance of a Lexicon

Linda Rudell-Betts, the expert who worked with Clear Channel to develop its lexicon, applies classic methods in approaching smart imaging. "With a digital image entry," she says, "what you have is the image information, the zeros and ones that make up a picture. Depending on what your recording device was, you may also have the date of the image capture, the JPEG number or file number that's automatically assigned, and perhaps some other capture data relating to exposures and settings. You have very little information telling you what the image is about; you don't know what you're looking at. The founding principles of the things we do in information science, the superset discipline over computer science and library science, go back three or four thousand years ago, to the library of Alexandria. I might use the word *hierarchy* or *taxonomy*, which is starting with a broad concept and going down to a narrower concept. You might have seen that on many web sites where they have a drop-down menu and you climb your way down a tree starting with a broad concept and going down to a narrow concept. That's a taxonomy, and it's the same thing as a biological taxonomy: vertebrates, mammals, primates, and on down the line. So, we start with a broad concept, getting ever narrower, and subdividing into very specific concepts."

Rudell-Betts continued, "Using really large collections, especially digital collections, where you don't have a physical set of items, if you had a set of folders, 20 or 30 physical folders sitting on your desk, you'd place your folders in certain piles. You have this spatial connection between this pile over here, which has all the interviews you've been working on, and this pile over here, which is the interviews you need to do. This pile over here is the bills you don't want to look at. So you've got a classification that is a physical classification—it's spatial. The same kind of classification works in a library, where you have books on a shelf. You know if you go to the area in the back of the library, where it says '900' on the side, that's where the biographies are (and usually there's a sign that says 'Biography' just to help people out), and so you just go there. That is an instance of classification in a physical environment. You take that into a digital environment, there is no 'place' to go to. All the data are on a server somewhere. They might have an arbitrary session number. The first item you put in may be called '001,' the second '002,' and so on. Now how does a user find that? With digital objects, be they images or text, when we feed them into a database we'll put them into specific fields."

Determining what those fields were and how they identified the Clear Channel images was Rudell-Betts's challenge.

Rudell-Betts reviewed the method she used to organize the lexicon: "The issue with Clear Channel was that they had images that you could look at in two different ways. One way is, *here is a product*. Their product is a lollipop billboard, an ad shell, or a bus wrap—any one of those things. It's an image of the product. Then, going in one dimension further, *what is the product displaying?* What is the 'aboutness' of the advertisement—what is the ad *about?* You have a bus that's advertising the [Los Angeles] Dodgers—that's always my all-time favorite one—where an image of the whole team is wrapped on a bus, and you see the Dodgers go by. So you have the Dodgers on the MTA bus; then you have the Dodgers on billboards; then you have the Dodgers on bus stops. Those are three different things, but they all have the same subject. That was the first thing to do, to discriminate between these two things, because their salespeople needed to be able to group together all the bus wraps and all the billboards and be able to pull up all the images that had to do with sports teams.

"In setting up the lexicons, the first thing we wanted to do was to organize all the different kinds of displays that they had. We gathered all the materials the salespeople had when they went out and did their pitch, from the 30- by 60-foot billboards all the way down to the little road signs, as well as all the wraps and the outdoor furniture, like bus-stop benches. All those had to be classified so that if the salespeople wanted to start at a very high level—'Show me all the outdoor media'—they'd get all the billboards, from something you'd see on Sunset Boulevard to something on a street corner reminding you that there was a cat show coming up this week."

Rudell-Betts observed that the human factor was one of the most important elements in building a user-friendly lexicon. "Another consideration when we're dealing with information retrieval is that people might have three or four different ways of describing their products. It was important for the lexicon to include all the variations.

Then we came to the subject—what was the aboutness of the particular advertisements? And for that there were three or four different subject headings that had been in use by different groups—the salespeople, the creative people—and then standard terms that the industry used. What I did with those was find all the commonalities and merged all the different languages and then came up with what made most sense, what was the closest to what they were accustomed to using. It's very important to get buy-in and to have respect for the vocabularies that these people have built up over the years. It is relevant because it arises from the organization. If the sales or creative people come to the Digital Image Library, they don't want to spend a whole lot of time thinking about where they're going; that's not their business. It's my business to help them get to where they need to go, as fast as possible. You want to keep the learning curve really low. The goal is, if one of the salespeople came in and said, 'I need to be able to find something about tennis shoes,' it would be flipped into an 'athletic shoes' search. The lexicon is set up so that that's possible."

Rudell-Betts passed on this advice to us: "Since you're writing for business readers, I'd like to emphasize the importance of having input from the people who will be using the system. In this case, Russ Mason created helpful glossaries describing what the images were about, the different display types, and in what cases they were used. He had a very good grasp of all that, and that made it very easy to work with him. Lexicons and taxonomies are all living and breathing entities that need to be updated; so if someone is planning a digital records system for images or text, or any media, they need to include in their business plan the maintenance of the subject indexing as a line item every bit as much as they need to upgrade their operating systems. There needs to be a repository of new terms and somebody assigned to regularly review the index and keep it up-to-date."

Russ Mason pointed out that Clear Channel's lexicon was so complete that "the Outdoor Advertising Association of America has adopted it for use as the industry standard. We figured if we built it and put it out there, other people would not want to reinvent the wheel. They would take it and use it, and the industry organization picked it up immediately." That's all part of the process. As smart standards emerge in any field, it becomes easier and more economical for companies to establish their own smart archives. The more you apply a systems approach to smart imaging, the more you have a basis from which to build the archive into the future, through changes in the business and changes in technology.

Having built the lexicon, Clear Channel needed a way of adding the data to the images to make them smart, with as little drudgery as possible, so they built a software application, called POP Prep. It's simple enough for anyone in a typical office to use. Employing a series of preset pop-up screens, the user can go into the lexicon, highlight the correct keywords, and attach those keywords to that image in the database to make them searchable. In large-market offices, assistants process the images; in smaller markets, the person who does the photography, often a sales or marketing rep, does the processing. The images are tagged immediately after capture, at the very beginning of the data chain, using the corporate-wide file-naming system, which includes structure number, advertiser, location, display format, product or service category, approach shot or close-up, and date. They are then uploaded to the local server to be immediately accessed by the various systems. More smart data is added as the image develops a history in the system.

IMPLEMENTING IN THE FIELD

A field implementation plan should address both equipment and training issues.

Equipment

Mason was responsible for equipping and training everyone who was out in the field capturing images. He told us, "I do all the research, set the company standards, and purchase all the digital cameras and related accessories from a local supplier I've been using for many years. I make the decisions based on matching the needs in the field to the capabilities of cameras and related accessories." Mason purchased more than 200 high-end consumer digital cameras for photographing structures and locations in the United States. These were 3.4- to 5-megapixel models with extended zoom capabilities to capture images of structures at great distances. The 60 information technology regionals each received midlevel 2- to 3-megapixel point-and-shoot consumer cameras. All the IT people in the field have cameras that they use to report Clear Channel site conditions from all over the United States.

Training

Clear Channel implemented a training program to help its photographers learn the digital work flow. "I trained over 200 photographers and 60 IT people over about a six- to seven-month period," Mason said. "This involved a half dozen one-day training sessions in different parts of the nation. Attendees ran the whole gamut, from photographers that we have on staff to the marketing, creative, and office people that end up doing the shooting. Some people had basic point-and-shoot skills and that's it. We did a morning hands-on training session on the cameras, and then in the afternoon we did a training session on the POP Prep system. Then they had to take the cameras out in the field and learn how to use them for our specific purposes. Once we placed the digital cameras out in the field, it took just a couple of months to get everyone in all the U.S. markets up to speed. One of the important things that we discovered during the training process was that the digital cameras produce a time stamp embedded in the image file that records exactly when the image was shot. When we compared the time stamp to the shooting logs, we found that some of the photographers weren't working as efficiently as they could. That time stamp helped us analyze and improve some of the work-flow issues out in the field and has also become a key part of the information we pass on to the clients as part of the POP document."

This automatic time stamp is the precursor to other technologies, which we cover in Chapter 8, aimed at automating and accelerating the smart image process. These smart, text-tagged images are immediately uploaded into the system, making them accessible to the Community of Interest the same day they are captured.

STEP 4. TRACK AND EVALUATE

Imaging at Clear Channel measures up to a criterion suggested by former Apple Computer CEO John Sculley in regard to measuring when a new technology was taking hold: "When a new technology becomes an everyday part of people's work flows, when its use is constant rather than occasional, then it's important from a business point of view."

Russ Mason agreed, "We use images constantly, every day, because of the speed and accuracy with which our infrastructure allows us to find and send images to people anytime, anywhere. For example, just today an account rep in Cleveland e-mailed us and said, 'I need a picture of location such-and-such and I need it right now. The client's coming through the door!' We found it and zapped it to him in less than two minutes. We see e-mails all the time from people working together around the world. By sending a global e-mail, I can contact all 80 creative people and all 50 marketing managers in the United States. Plus, it goes to people from the mall and AdShel divisions, airports, the taxis division, Times Square Spectacolor in New York, and to an international list. The distribution and use of images just constantly goes on."

Each of the internal constituencies in the Clear Channel Community of Interest benefits from the use of images. Of the 3,800 people in the outdoor division, Mason estimated about half in some way come in contact with these images—either by creating them, viewing them, referencing them, or attaching them to a document. "The size of the office affects that answer," Mason said. "We have about 100 people here in Los Angeles, and at least half of them in one way or another touch those images, while in our San Diego office, where there are only six or seven—mostly salespeople—I'd say 100 percent of them do." The images flow inside and outside the company to an extensive community.

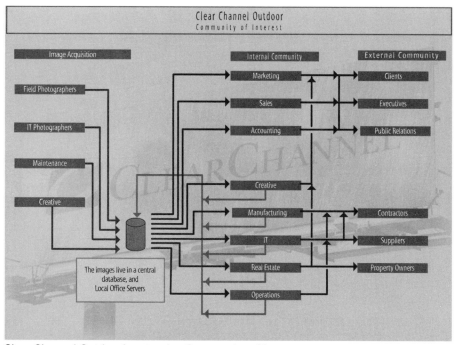

Clear Channel Outdoor's extensive Community of Interest

We reviewed with Russ Mason a representative sampling of ways in which Clear Channel is *Going Visual.*

Maintenance

"Our photographers are like the eyes that are out there in the field," Mason said. "Sometimes they'll go out to photograph and see something's wrong, like graffiti or damage to the structure or trees that are growing in the way or some other problem. I tell our photographers to shoot one frame and then note on their log what the problem is, and we'll send that to the operations manager, who uses the picture to get the right people out there to take care of it. In addition, all the maintenance crews have cameras in their trucks in case they come across a problem at a site. We always send images to the tree-trimming supervisor, who e-mails it to his crew so they can tell the amount of time it's going to take, how big the crew has to be—they can estimate what they'll need to do the job. Then they take a picture when they're finished to show it's done, and that's how they get

Graffiti damage

paid." Because all the structures are archived in the database, these maintenance issues and their solutions become part of the recorded history of each structure.

IT

All information-technology field technicians have digital cameras and use them to visually communicate problems and challenges to their supervisors. "The IT people are big on images," said Mason. "They all have cameras, and they service all the divisions, the radio stations, television stations, entertainment offices, and interactive offices. They can go into a radio station and see a problem, take a photograph of it, and e-mail it right back to company headquarters in San Antonio with a message saying, 'We've got this problem; we need help.' If it has to do with cabling, it goes off to the people in charge of that; if they need additional equipment, it goes to purchasing; and so on. As company acquisitions were made, we had to standardize all the computer systems across the country. These pictures give us a clear idea of what's there, what else we need, and where it's supposed to go—all before we walk in the door."

Real Estate Management

"We shoot locations for the real estate department," Mason said, "because if they go lease a piece of land, they want to show the person we're leasing that land from what the structure is going to look like. We provide a previsualization. If that was my property across the street and Clear Channel was proposing putting a pole right there to support a structure, I would want to know what it's going to look like. So we shoot the location, then come back and drop an image of the structure, measured to scale, so it looks exactly like the real thing. So we can negotiate with the owner by image to

Proposed property

Previsualized

arrive at an acceptable situation, then we get approval and sign the lease."

Sales

"Those same photographs are also used to presell that location. When you want to sell that space to an advertiser, you want to show them—here's what this location is going to look like in 60 days when the billboard is in place."

Creative

Open access to the database gives the creatives a vast repository of historical display references, current displays, and actual source material such as royalty-free images, logos, and fonts, which are used to generate new advertisements.

Clients

"Images are critical to our relationship with the clients, says Mason. "The marketing and salespeople are constantly interacting with the agencies, media-buying services, and advertisers using images. All sales sheets are image-centric, showing creative examples or specific location examples. Images are used to show the clients what their ads will look like in the locations being proposed. In many cases, a 'post-buy analysis' is done by the client and given to the client to show a history of this particular media buy. The analysis is broken into sections described as The Problem, The Plan, The Results, and The Client's Response, and that will have all the contracts, all the Proof of Performance photographs in it."

The Fast Pitch system promotes very effective communication with the clients. Mason told us: "The clients are just blown away. They can't believe the quality and the speed of the proposals. What has always been difficult, when you have multiple offices across the nation, is putting a multimarket proposal together. With Fast Pitch, when we need to put the top five markets together for a presentation, to get all the maps, all of the bulletin inventory sheets together, all the media kits together, all the product pages together, everything all in one package, now we can go online and do it all because everything is archived in the database."

Travel

In addition to all the visual marketing and sales material, the clients receive the critical Proof of Performance reports in which photographs of all the contracted locations verify that Clear Channel has fulfilled its commitments. There has been an evolution in the importance of the Proof of Performance system because the needs of the clients are changing. "For example," Mason observed, "because of economic conditions, many companies' travel budgets have been decreased. There used to be, and there still is to a certain degree, a group of people called *riders,* whom clients employ to come to a market and ride a showing; in other words, they ride around to see all the billboard locations. But now, with people not traveling as much, the clients are relying much more on viewing photographs of the locations from our archive, and they're more interested in what their ad looks like as you're approaching it from the car's viewing angle. We're saving them time and money by photographing in a way that eliminates the need for them to send people around the country. We're satisfying the needs of our customers based on the fact that we've established that we can communicate visually in this way, and by making that visual communication available to them."

Approach shot   Close-up

Marketing

The marketing department people use the system to prepare materials using data from the various image-storage and asset systems to support sales and public relations efforts. The Market View system enables them to coordinate efforts nationwide by giving them a complete visual record of any ad campaign.

Operations

Display installers are given photos in order to plan for crew size, time, and special equipment needed for particularly challenging installations.

Pictures are taken of equipment for inventory purposes. When structural changes are made to a piece of equipment—an installation truck, for example—its condition is documented when it comes into the shop and then again when it's finished, and those images go into the database. These pictures are used as references if the shop needs to replicate a specific configuration.

Customized installation truck

Manufacturing

Images flow from the creative group to the manufacturing group for the production of the displays. Manufacturing specifications are on the Clear Channel web site, and clients can use images to previsualize their displays according to those specs.

Accounting

The invoice on every account is accompanied by the image-verified Proof of Performance document.

Executive

The marketing department prepares extensive visual outdoor advertising histories of long-running, brand-name accounts, which are assembled in book form and presented by Clear Channel's CEO to the client's CEO. The top executives know that because of the smart imaging strategy's Market View component, they can review an entire account's history, including all the locations and creative examples, quickly and easily to prepare for client meetings.

Public Relations

Key images from high-profile and pro bono public-service campaigns provide the visual elements for Clear Channel's public relations efforts.

The *Going Visual* strategy has proven critical to the entire Community of Interest. The system has been designed such that each individual image must be accessible to everyone for any use at any time. The experience has to be easy, transparent, and completely dependable. With proper planning and disciplined execution, the competitive rewards of a system like Clear Channel's are immense. Russ Mason says, "No other company even comes close to having a system like ours."

STEP 5. REASSESS AND EDUCATE

The success of Clear Channel's *Going Visual* strategy has led to greater demands on the system. More images are being created daily, and more innovative uses for images are constantly being invented. An expansion of hardware and software is necessary to keep up with the community's appetite for visual information.

Tomorrow the World

Clear Channel has more than 750,000 display surfaces around the world and is working on capturing smart images of all of those so that the entire inventory will be accessible from the archive. The company currently has photo servers in all of its 56 U.S. offices, and is currently capturing and adding to the database an average of more than 27,000 images a month. A standardized database of smart images enables anyone in the system to know exactly how to search any of those servers.

Panoramic and Video

Mason has experimented with interactive 360-degree panorama shots known as VR (short for virtual reality), which allow the viewer to look around an entire space in one interactive image. "We have some VR on our web site; it's good for specialty-type things," he said. "We've shot VR in Chicago, in the North Western train station and in the subway system, to give people a feeling for what this is, because it's something different. We also went up to Toronto, Canada, to Dundas Square and Eaton Center, where we have turned the whole sides of the mall into huge outdoor displays. Inside of the Eaton Center, there are humongous ads hung from the ceilings that we shot in panoramic VR. As a marketing test, we shot a VR in our own large-format printing department to give clients a feel for that facility online. There are other specialty niches where we could use VR, in malls and airports, places where we control 360 degrees of space."

Mason is also evaluating the use of live video: "We are exploring installing live video feeds on selected displays. A number of our clients have expressed a need to see their displays on a daily basis. Some of the campaigns, timed to the release schedule of a movie or the airing of a TV show, change on a faster cycle than the traditional monthly run. We have been researching Internet-connected wireless webcams that are capable of high enough image quality to satisfy the client. The client will be able to directly access the webcam at each location and see a live image. There is no end to the possibilities."

Possibilities like this, for high-quality, remote-location image capture, are driving developments that, according to Nikon's Jerry Grossman, will "enable people to wirelessly control their camera's functions and transfer their images directly to printers, computers, or the network. Positioning the camera, focusing, zooming, and triggering image capture can all be done by a remote connection. When these capabilities are combined with the ability to wirelessly transfer the files, it allows for the useful placement of cameras in physical locations that have been inaccessible up to now. Wireless really changes the game."

Expanding to Other Media

As we pointed out at the opening of this chapter, we focused on Clear Channel's outdoor division because that is where the company's *Going Visual* strategy took root. Mason is hard at work bringing other divisions and other media into the system: "We have sections for international outdoor, a section for domestic outdoor, malls, a section for taxis," he said. "Then we're getting ready to talk to the radio and the television people. We have to do this as an evolution because it takes terabytes of storage. The television division, for example, could access video segments through our archiving system. That's what we're proposing." Once an enterprise has established the smart archive and the community has embraced its value, there are no limits to the archive's innovative, functional uses.

PRACTICAL EXERCISE

Use pictures to generate a trip report. Whether you're going to a trade show, out on a sales call, or visiting a factory, use images to

show rather than tell. Take photos of customers and their environments. The visual knowledge gained will enhance interpersonal relations by giving a richer context to phone and e-mail relationships.

Kodak's Jim Stoffel, who travels the world overseeing work groups
and facilities that develop imaging products and services, offered
this advice, "As you might imagine, I take a lot of pictures on business trips. We have a multinational R&D operation, and I am
always taking pictures of the new team or a new company that we're
working with. It really helps the teams in Europe, the United States,
or the Far East to see pictures of who is working in a particular lab
or manufacturing site. It builds a relationship that transcends the
written monthly report, with its 20 pages of text and graphs showing how many parts they produced last month. Also, when you try
to describe, 'here's the layout for this new manufacturing line; here's
what it looks like,' there is nothing like a picture. Describing a
20,000-foot clean room with a photograph is very effective, allowing
you to provide quality communication on a technical level. There is
no language issue."

CHAPTER 7

Being There by *Going Visual*

The bedrock goal of any *Going Visual* strategy is to increase the value of interpersonal communication. To this point we have focused our attention primarily on transforming the written word to visual images. In this chapter we explore the effect of adding the visual component to spoken words by transforming telephone calls into video calls. Humankind has long desired to see remote locations, to project our vision into spaces where we are not physically present. The experience or impression of being present at a location remote from one's own actual physical environment is called *telepresence,* and its most common application is called *videoconferencing.*

Our research shows us that imaging and telecommunication are converging technologically to enable people in distant locations to converse and collaborate in ways that include virtually the full spectrum of interactions individuals experience when they are in the same location. Whether via computer-based videoconferencing or video-enabled camera phones, telepresence is becoming a mainstream business tool.

In this chapter we describe how a global corporation is making use of today's visual-information tools on an everyday basis. This enterprise has adopted videoconferencing to facilitate the decision-making process for project-based groups whose members are based in different organizations throughout the company and in different locations around the globe. To adequately describe the full potential of telepresence, we also introduce you to researchers at MIT's Human Connectedness project, who are doing the pioneering work of understanding the interaction between the technology and the human factors involved.

Videoconferencing as a practical reality is generally viewed as having had a checkered history. First introduced to the U.S. public in the 1960s and promoted through the 1990s in the form of personal videophones, the technology was saddled with poor picture quality and the prerequisite of buying expensive, matching equipment on both ends of the conversation in order to send and receive image and voice. Consumers resisted videophones for social reasons, such as a fear of allowing people to see how they look when they wake up. As in everything else related to *Going Visual*, videoconferencing began to become a viable option when it migrated into the digital realm, where it partnered well with computers, videocams, and the Internet. For most companies today, the promise of videoconferencing is thus far just that, all promise—a potentially powerful form of communication that hasn't reached the cost-benefit tipping point for adoption. However, as with most everything else related to *Going Visual*, videoconferencing is quickly moving toward an ease of use and cost model that will make it possible for any business to adopt. It can be as simple as two people viewing each other on computer monitors (or, in some parts of the world, on camera phones) or as complex as multiple individuals and groups interacting with each other on large-screen displays.

Innovative companies, like the one that provides this chapter's story, make extensive use of videoconferencing to manage teams that involve people in offices and on project sites around the world. These teams use the system to plan and execute projects by making direct voice and visual contact with each other, while simultaneously viewing and collaborating on the supporting information in the form of the documents, images, videos, and presentations that they need to make decisions.

Please meet one of the leaders of the corporate videoconferencing vanguard, Jim O'Leary, real-time collaboration project manager for a major international entertainment company that prefers to remain unnamed. This global enterprise is involved in all aspects of media production and distribution, and it builds and operates theme parks around the world. At O'Leary's company, everyday operations involve the management of complex projects by individuals and groups working together from different locations. While these individuals are tasked with accomplishing specific goals by working together, in what O'Leary calls "virtual teams," they rarely, if ever, all meet in person. He describes how videoconferencing has become the essential communication medium for managing projects worldwide.

DEFINING THE VALUE PROPOSITION: TRAVEL

"The first thing people mention when they consider videoconferencing," according to O'Leary, "is, 'We can save travel dollars and we can save time away from the office.' That is certainly part of the equation. People who keep track of it show good returns on investment, probably more than they expected. When I was having discussions with any of our CIOs [chief information officers] or CTOs [chief technology officers] across the company, I would ask them, 'How often do you travel, and why?' A typical answer was, 'Right now I make a trip around the world to all of our locations five to six times a year. With videoconferencing, I'd probably travel only four times a year.' A reduction of one trip may not seem like much until you do the math: That's a 16 to 20 percent savings, at a time when organizations are overjoyed to find cost reductions in the single digits.

DEFINING THE VALUE PROPOSITION: BEYOND TRAVEL

The benefits of implementing telepresence technology, however, go much deeper than cost savings in one area. They relate to a piece of an organization's core values—productivity and operating culture. O'Leary observed, "Not only do executives spend less time and money on travel, they keep in tighter contact with their colleagues at the remote locations, make decisions more quickly, and come to conclusions more readily. It doesn't just accelerate the way that you do business; it *changes* the way that you do business, the way that you make decisions. It allows you to reach out and include individuals from scattered parts of the company to collaborate and to help make decisions."

O'Leary recalled that the early adopters were virtual teams whose needs drove the initial implementation of the technology. "They were looking for whatever means they could to stay on track," he said. "There may be individuals who are personally resistant to that, but as a whole, those groups were the first to latch on. One of the first to come on board was our international construction group, because they're building theme parks around the world and are being directed by a central creative and strategic management group. Typically, a videoconference for one of their projects will include project managers, creative staff members, architects—all the people who are making critical decisions about where the projects are going."

While these project-based virtual teams have led the charge in adopting telepresence technology, videoconferencing has quickly caught on in other areas of the company. "From a corporate perspective," O'Leary said, "you've got IT, finance, and HR organizations scattered throughout the company. As our company and so many others are having all of these key service segments organized into single global departments, they have to keep in communication with each other, and videoconferencing provides the crucial link." The effect on human resources is particularly notable, with videoconferencing beginning to have a profound effect on training and on hiring practices.

"Training organizations have long been oriented toward stand-up training, theater-led training," said O'Leary. "Then they went through a spell of computer-based training, which proved unsatisfactory for a lot of folks. What they're coming back to is live, web-based training in which an expert or several experts appear online, participating and presenting their piece of the training. You can involve these experts from wherever they are and make them real people, relevant participants who have something important to say, and that is effective and attention getting. You can have the most valuable person for this particular training, and you don't have to fly them in and pay for hotels and rental cars. These 'virtual training' facilities change the whole nature of the process."

Videoconferencing's effect on hiring practices has been profound. O'Leary explained: "I've noticed that we now have a tendency to find people where they are, and not relocate them as much as we used to. Because of the richness of modern communications, you use people where they are, for their talents and for the time period that you need them, and you don't relocate them. You don't necessarily colocate them in a field office because you can 'virtually' colocate them for whatever task you need." Videoconferencing has had a major impact in hiring this new generation of employees, for whom this technology is an essential component, a requirement, in fact, of their business lifestyle.

O'Leary stressed that beyond the way in which the communicative powers of videoconferencing are now being put to use in many divisions of the company, the technology has become an important link between the divisions, the glue of the company. "When I think about HR, finance, IT, and construction," O'Leary said, "all of the different areas of expertise that are using these same-time but long-distance videoconferencing tools, I ask, 'What's the common thread between them?' It's project management; they've got something big to do. They have to coordinate people and resources and activities in order to complete a job, and that requires that everybody be on the same page, and there's not a lot of time to be wasted in getting everyone on the same page. So in my mind, that's been one of the key reasons for the success of videoconferencing. A team can look back and say, we had something big to do and we could not have achieved it without videoconferencing."

As the use of videoconferencing has begun to spread throughout the organization, valuable lessons have been learned about its effectiveness. It turns out that different aspects of the tool matter under different circumstances, and in some cases it's not the right tool at all.

DEFINING THE VALUE PROPOSITION:
HUMAN CONNECTEDNESS AND TRUST

For some executives, typically of senior rank within an organization, the most important aspect of videoconferencing is simple face-to-face interaction—what O'Leary called "a talking head." "Video-conferencing by itself seems to work best for folks like top executives who are dealing primarily with trust issues," said O'Leary. "For instance, you've got a VP and a senior VP who are in different parts of the country. They're working out a strategy that revolves around deciding what needs to be done, when it needs to be done, and who needs to take responsibility for it. That is not presentation-oriented. It's sitting as if you're in the same room, talking back and forth and working things out. You can do that over the phone, if you've previously established a trusting relationship in person. But if you've never had the opportunity to sit down with someone, or that initial opportunity was very brief, videoconferencing can give you many of these in-person elements and enable you to build that trust.

"In my own case," O'Leary continued, "there are people I know quite well whom I've never met in person. There's a guy on my team that I work with every day; I've never met him in person, but I feel just as if I had because I've sat in the same virtual room with him so many times. Through conversation, through eye contact, through the typical things that you have to do together to get things done, you build trust. That experience of establishing trust also extends to group dynamics, to how people act around their superiors, equals, or subordinates. That tells you a lot about a person. When you've got groups of people that may be communicating with one another about sensitive things, it's important to be aware of exactly who is on the other end of the conversation. Who has walked in or out of the room? You want to know, who's really there? Which means you have to see it."

DEFINING THE VALUE PROPOSITION: BEYOND THE TALKING HEADS

In many cases, however, videoconferencing as an effective tool for these groups goes beyond merely seeing a live video image of another person—the so-called talking head. While expressions and body language are always valuable, the greatest benefit accrues by holding a virtual working session, to view, interact with, and iterate together all the visual and text-based information that would be part of any in-person business meeting—documents, images, videos, presentations, and demonstrations of new equipment or software.

Microsoft's Amir Majdamehr commented on the importance using voice and video when sharing documents from remote locations, "Because of the advent of networking, people in large companies are spread out, and there is a need to disseminate information to them. Our focus for the enterprise is understanding what information knowledge workers need to convey to others in their corporation that are not colocated with them, and what tools and technologies they need in order to do that successfully. In the old days, if you had a new product, you would print out brochures and have people fly in for meetings. Today, telepresence is a way to provide that information remotely. When we look at the triangle of tools the knowledge worker has—PowerPoint, Word, and Excel—the question is, how can we add a fourth leg that creates new opportunities and make the users' lives easier? Audio, video, and imaging are the things we need to bring together as that fourth leg. The typical PowerPoint experience is a series of slides, but without the person talking over them, it is not a self-describing document. What really gives that presentation impact is the human voice that explains what the presentation is all about. It turns out the face also adds value in that it adds interest and emotion. PowerPoint is basically very static information that is not complete, but adding audio to it increases the information content substantially. And then if you add video to it, it becomes a completely invigorated experience. Not as good as being there, but it is the next best thing."

"What really works," said O'Leary, "is combining the talking heads—the visual cues and facial expressions that would be part of the information flow in a face-to-face meeting—with the data that would be shared in such a meeting. For instance, I might have a spreadsheet or a word document or a PowerPoint presentation, and the excitement that you can read in my face and my voice, along with the words on the page, have a much larger impact and can more effectively communicate the importance of any particular thing than voice or words alone. The video aspect of this just increases communication. It makes it possible for everyone on the project team to stay in sync as to the progress of the project and for each individual to quickly communicate, with the full power of visual cues, to the entire team. We've found that as you move into the detail aspect of the projects, the importance of the talking heads is even less. What's important is the live, dynamic, real-time data exchange. We're working on the same document, separated by distance but not by time."

Increasingly, these documents themselves involve visual elements. In addition to spreadsheets, word documents, and slides, O'Leary noted the proliferation of "video clips and pictures taken with digital cameras. The things that in the past would have arrived the next day by overnight delivery are now being shared directly, in real time . . . any medium that visually describes the work that is being done or the plans for the work that is going to be done."

DEFINING THE VALUE PROPOSITION: WHAT DOESN'T WORK

As essential as videoconferencing can be in the situations just described, it does not necessarily add value to more mundane meetings. O'Leary explained: "Some organizations whose members are located in different parts of the company have looked at this as, 'We can have our staff meetings by videoconference.' They tried it a couple of times, and they concluded that, you know what? After the initial excitement of it, who cares? A simple staff meeting, for a team in which everyone knows each other, giving the status of what's going on in your little neck of the woods might as well all be on a voice conference, or the group members can all submit their status reports by worksheet or e-mail. That really isn't a strong case for videoconferencing. For teams, it works best when there's urgency, when there's something to accomplish in a time-sensitive way."

IMPLEMENTATION: PERSONAL VERSUS GROUP VIDEOCONFERENCES

Paralleling the different-use cases explored so far, deploying the systems throughout a large organization requires a mix of individual and group installations. Decisions regarding the mix should be subject to a cost-versus-needs analysis. "Typically, if you're an executive, you either have your own personal videoconference room or a video-conference set within your office," said O'Leary, "and there is a growing demand for that. If you're a staff member, then there's a videoconference room down the hallway. Each videoconferencing set that sits on the network, no matter if it's a room-based system or a personal system, draws pretty much the same amount of network bandwidth."

To ensure that everyone has the appropriate system to get the job done, O'Leary's team deployed several options. "We've developed a concept of videoconferencing around medium-sized conference rooms where the capital investment is about $20,000. That includes a couple of large-screen displays—one for the video, one for the PC—an in-room PC that's always there, and the ability to log on to the corporate network from your laptop so you can bring your work in. Someone can bring their presentation on their own laptop and share that, or they can fire up the in-room PC and log on to their own network drive." Access to the supporting information, whether it is from an individual participant's laptop or from the company's image and document archives, is essential for the success of the videoconference.

"As more and more people started hearing about how effective these videoconferences were," O'Leary said, "work groups started coming to us, saying, 'We need to communicate more regularly with our counterparts in this location and that location, and we're not able to book the conference room, and we don't have the money to spend on outfitting another conference room—what can you do for us?' One alternative solution we've devised is a videoconferencing system set on a mobile cart. It moves around between offices and small conference rooms and gives a lot more flexibility. Now, it's not the right kind of set for groups of 15 to 20 people. It's good for groups of three to five, and your investment is $5,000 to $7,000 versus $20,000. The groups have come back and said, 'This is great, we like this.' "

What does the experience of participating in one of these video-conferences actually feel like? Videoconferences frequently have three or four different sources, or nodes, which may consist of a group in Florida, another group in France, an individual in California, and an individual in Illinois. The system has to be flexible enough to display the people and information on the screen in as natural a way as possible so that a productive conversation can take place. O'Leary described the arrangement: "Basically, it's a split-screen. If you have three nodes that are in conversation, you'll have two nodes toward the top and one at the bottom. If four nodes come on, then it'll be a *Hollywood Squares* kind of thing. Occasionally there are some conferences where you'll have seven, eight, nine sites participating, and since each roomful of people is represented by one of nine windows, and these windows have gotten pretty small, each person in that window is a tiny speck on the screen. You can't even see their eyebrows, and that defeats the whole purpose. So you set up the videoconferencing system in what's called 'presentation mode,' and whoever is speaking becomes the presenter. The multipoint control unit, which is the centralized management hardware and software, figures out who's speaking and where the audio is coming from, and makes that the large screen on everyone else's video.

"We use standard, off-the-shelf software to accomplish this, and everyone in the system uses the same setup. For the individual users working from their own remote locations, we specify the standards and configuration of their system, and they are responsible for buying and setting up their equipment. The standardization is important because, from an enterprise point of view, we want to have consistency and manageability. I want to be able to know who is using the system, track their calls, build call-detail reports, and provide a global address directory that's consistent for everyone. With this system in place, initiating a videoconference can be as simple as this: Schedule a room that has videoconferencing equipment in it, walk in, pick up the remote, open the directory page, select an entry and make the call."

Recent technology developments, in the form of inexpensive webcams producing high-quality images, have enabled O'Leary's organization to extend the visual capabilities of the system by including always-on, live, remote visual information direct from a project site. O'Leary said, "Videoconference sessions often involve a project group reporting their progress to management by showing some representative pictures. Webcams are starting to get integrated to the point where they're almost as good as business-oriented systems; the video quality is actually pretty phenomenal. So we have started installing webcams, connected to the network, at some of the building sites. The result has been that the reporting structure has changed from 'We'll give you a monthly progress update' to 'We have the webcams on our intranet, and via a web page you can see the progress anytime for yourself.'

"The webcam saves a picture every five minutes. So you can look over the past hour, or the past five days, or the past five months if you want to, and get a visual record of the project's progress. That changes the nature of the business communication, because when you're sitting down with your managers and giving a status report, you don't necessarily have to gather up all this information or physically send someone out to the project site. You just go to the web site that holds this webcam's set of pages and find the representative pages that show progress."

Archiving these images is an automated process. Because critical, fixed information (e.g., location and project number) can be set on the camera, and because other important identifiers (e.g., time and date) are automatically stamped on the file electronically, these webcams create valuable information assets on the fly. As O'Leary described, "The basic archival mechanisms are no more complex than generating images and storing them to an assigned folder on the network. A simple script reviews the folders every week and deletes information that is older than a specified date."

In a business structure that includes virtual teams, well-organized and designed videoconferencing can be a vital part of a *Going Visual* strategy.

TELEPRESENCE: THE NEXT GENERATION

The availability of inexpensive webcams and the broadband Internet access used by more and more businesses set the stage for a type of persistent, or always-on, telepresence. This notion of a system that is always on is at the heart of one of the simplest, most effective examples we've ever seen of the potential of telepresence to go beyond today's implementations and fundamentally restructure the way businesses communicate. Deep and complex theories lie behind the example we're about to describe, but the practical reality is as familiar as bumping into a colleague at the watercooler. We call this experience "The Tale of Two Couches."

The common area at the MIT Media Lab in Cambridge, Massachusetts, can be adequately depicted only in images, but confidentiality requirements prevent that, so we ask that you visualize a wild assemblage of computer workstations, tables covered with pieces of devices being built into Rube Goldberg contraptions, and cameras and monitors everywhere.

The ceiling at the time of our visit was a maze of tracks from which hung tiny cameras, each attached to its own miniature server. The cameras were all networked together so that a viewer could follow the movement of anyone who passed through the space. In the middle of the room was a big black couch. When we sat on the couch, we noticed that projected on an 8- by 6-foot area on the wall in front of us was a video image of us on the couch, along with three other images, forming a grid of four. One of the other images was of another couch, very much like the one we were sitting on, only that one was located 3,000 miles away in the MIT Media Lab Europe, in Dublin. The other two screens were outdoor images of the skylines of Dublin and Cambridge, respectively.

Media Labs connected in Cambridge and Dublin

Michael Bove, the MIT professor who was our guide, explained that this was an always-on system whose user interface consisted of simply sitting on the couch and touching a button to activate the voice component of the communication. The reason for the images of the outdoors was to provide a casual conversation starter, so someone sitting on the couch in Cambridge might quip to a colleague in Dublin, "Oh, you have a sunny day there today," and get the conversation started in a very minimal way. The elements of this system couldn't be simpler: at each location, a small webcam and a tiny microphone directed at the couch, another webcam perched outside, all connected to the network, and a video projector. By sitting on either couch, you, in effect, enter a transatlantic common area where you might meet anyone in the organization who happened by, or you might arrange to meet someone at the couch for a face-to-face meeting. Because of the five-hour time difference, no one happened to be in the Dublin lab while we passed through Cambridge, but even seeing an empty couch was evocative and useful. It made the time difference feel more tangible by confirming that no one was there. We mentioned to Bove that we were planning a trip to the Dublin site, and he urged us to meet with his colleague in residence there, Stefan Agamanolis, to learn more about the concepts behind this system.

Dr. Stefan Agamanolis

Several months later we arrived at the beautiful old former Guinness brewing building that houses the MIT Media Lab Europe. The heavy stone walls and thick plank floors, which used to hold kegs of Ireland's finest brew, now glowed in the soft light of computer and TV screens. Dr. Stefan Agamanolis, principal research scientist of the Human Connectedness group, greeted us and immediately, and we sat on the very same couch we had last viewed from across the Atlantic. On a large projection screen attached to a rough brick wall, we saw the same grid of four scenes we'd viewed in Cambridge. When we expressed our interest in his approach to this project, Agamanolis launched right into it: "This project demonstrates some important concepts about my research, which is about *connectedness,* a word which has become almost a buzzword for us. The idea here is to go beyond mere connections—telephone calls, e-mails, that kind of thing—and engage the periphery of human sensations: background communication and background cues. When people come in and see this project, they think videoconferencing; they think this is an always-on videoconference. But that's the wrong starting point to understand what I'm trying to accomplish. There is in fact a conferencing mode. We can click a couple of buttons here and go into a videoconference with the people in the garden in Dublin, but the main purpose of this is to foster a sense of community, to give you the impression that there really is a window broken through this wall that is leading into another room, when in fact the room is actually 3,000 miles away. This makes people feel they are contributing to a larger whole by working along with a lot of other people who are not necessarily physically near.

"It's difficult to get across in a 30-minute demo really how much this installation has become a part of the fabric of our existence. This has been up and running for almost a year, and it's become so much a part of the background of our environment that we don't even think about it anymore. We walk by and we see the images on the screen, and we might notice someone on the other end that we know, or we just see people working in the background, or we see an empty room, or we see a large group of visitors going through, or someone sitting eating lunch, so we press the button and have a chance encounter with them. It's that ambient awareness that this system is trying to get at."

At that moment, we saw a couple of people enter the common area in Cambridge, and Agamanolis casually pressed the microphone button and said hello. It just so happened that the World Cup soccer matches were going on at the time, and the Cambridge crew had come in early to watch a game over the lab's high-speed Internet connection. The conversation was all about the American team's chances in the next round. We were astounded to see how natural the interaction was, as though everyone was in the same room, and we were reminded of an observation by Howard Rheingold, author of *Smart Mobs:*

> Whenever a new communication technology lowers the threshold for groups to act collectively, new kinds of institutions emerge. We are seeing the combination of network communications and social networks.

We see systems such as this one extending a *Going Visual* strategy into the Community of Interest in a rather profound way, by lowering the barriers of time and distance.

Videoconferencing for Everyone

While the requirements of O'Leary's organization are at the high end of the quality scale, the rapid democratization of technology involved in *Going Visual,* in terms of both price and ease of use, is changing who can play the game. The price/performance value of webcams now puts them within virtually anyone's reach. Technical standards have also been adopted that make basic videoconferencing easy to do on any modern PC, and O'Leary tells us that the full capabilities he's been describing are just around the corner for everyone. "A new set of protocols has just been adopted, called SIP, Session Initiation Protocol, which will greatly simplify things," he said. "The old protocols require a lot of processing power, and programming them is not for the faint of heart. So you've needed top-notch programmers

(Continued)

(Continued)

to build videoconferencing systems, and that means they've been built for corporate users, who can afford it. This new protocol will change videoconferencing from being a corporate phenomenon to being an everyman's tool. It lets a lot more people get into the business of videoconferencing, and it allows you to build applications much more cheaply. It allows you to buy fairly inexpensive webcams and use them to collaborate on your personal PC. It's going to allow videoconferencing to really take the place of picking up the phone."

To illustrate how far the democratization of videoconferencing has already come, we cite a scene we happened upon while researching this book. While sitting in a coffee shop, checking e-mail on a laptop through a wireless network, we noticed a young mom guide her stroller to a nearby table. She sat down, unpacked her laptop, clipped a small webcam to the top of its screen,

Coffee shop family videoconference

and plugged in a tiny pair of speakers. She then pulled out a makeup kit, applied lipstick and powder, and slipped on a pair of dangly earrings. After a final check in the mirror, she picked up her cell phone and called her husband to let him know she was ready to videoconference. Moments later, she pulled the baby up in her lap, and the three of them had a videoconference right there in the coffee shop. There was the baby waving to Dad, and Dad seeing and talking to the baby. He was in Colorado; she was in Los Angeles. Videoconferencing and a cup of coffee—this is an example of *Going Visual* right from the cradle.

PRACTICAL EXERCISE

Take a picture of something you don't know how to fix.

LightSurf's Philippe Kahn recalled how a picture helped fix a machine, "I was in a Kinko's late at night needing to make copies, and one of the big color photocopiers was down, and I saw that there was a technician on the floor, lying on his back under the unit, speaking to someone on his cell phone, trying to describe the machine's wiring. He was saying, 'I'm seeing there's this blue wire that's going from this to that, and a yellow wire here . . .' and it is obvious to me that he is having a hard time communicating what he's seeing, and he is not getting the answer he needs from the supervisor on the other end of the phone. I leaned down and asked him if the guy he was speaking to had an e-mail address. He said yes, and I handed him my camera phone and said, 'Try this.' The guy snapped a picture of the wires that he was seeing, sent it instantly over to the other guy, and a minute later, the supervisor was saying, 'Oh, you've got the model X3072. In that case, what you need to be doing is this and such.' The poor technician had been under the machine for goodness knows how long trying to solve this problem with words. With an image, it was fixed in a snap."

CHAPTER 8

Going Further Visual:
Five Future Steps

So far we've described how businesses can improve their operations by applying tools and technologies that all of us are already familiar with: digital, still, and video cameras; camera phones; computers; printers; and the Internet. As valuable as we've shown these to be, we have even better news (as they say in infomercials, "Wait, there's more!"): The next *five years* will see greater development of tools and infrastructures that enable visual communication than have been seen in the past *five centuries*.

Technology is being developed and deployed so quickly that a science fiction film like *Minority Report,* released in 2002, which showcases the everyday use of futuristic concepts 50 years in the future, is already being overtaken by reality. Its 3D holographic displays and electronic newspapers showing ever-changing text, still, and moving images represent technology that exists today and will be widely available within the next three years. As a result, the companies that invest today in integrating visual communication tools and practices into their work flow will find the advantage they gain immediately will become magnified in the future, as increasingly powerful tools allow them to derive even greater benefits from their initial investment in *Going Visual.*

FIVE DIRECTIONS FOR THE NEAR FUTURE

In this chapter we're going to tap into the knowledge we've gained from conversations and demonstrations with leading scientists, engineers, and entrepreneurs who are working on a broad spectrum of new technologies that will push the possibilities for visual communication far beyond what we think of today as "photography." We're going to introduce you to some of these people so that you can hear, directly from them, descriptions of the systems being built and deployed that will dramatically extend the visual communications potential we've begun to explore.

Five major themes emerged from these conversations, five directions that we believe imaging innovation will focus on during the next three to five years. Here's what we call them:

1. The imaging ecosystem

2. Visual mobility

3. Automatic imaging

4. Vivid imaging

5. Personalized authoring

Taken together, these five directions comprise a set of key interlocking concepts and technologies identified by the visual visionaries we interviewed as the foremost emerging strategies that mainstream businesses will adopt in the next three years.

THE ECOSYSTEM AND SMART DATA: MAKING THE PIECES FIT TOGETHER

One of the major challenges that average users have faced in trying to put technology to use, whether in their business or personal lives, is that, simply put, this stuff doesn't all work together. In earlier days, one company could confidently say, "You push the button and we do the rest." Today, however, the "stuff" that enables *Going Visual* is made and sold not just by different companies, but by companies that are in completely different businesses, ranging from imaging companies to cellular carriers, from information-processing companies and computer makers to consumer-electronics companies and more—it is a very long list. Today's technology customer has a legitimate expectation that the parts *should* all work together, and seamlessly at that. Regardless of whether they are in the same or different industries, headquartered on the same city block or across the globe, it is the responsibility of the companies who make these products to ensure that users are never left scratching their heads, stalled because the technology is too difficult to manage. In the technology business, the answer to that requirement is *standards,* meaning common specifications that all companies agree to implement so that their products do, indeed, work together seamlessly.

Significant progress in standards development has been made in the past 10 years; in fact, a key reason that visual communication works as well as it does in the Communities of Interest we've described in previous chapters is the adoption of imaging standards that allow for the capture, editing, transfer, and viewing of images in formats universal to all of the links in the information chain. Going forward, as the types of multimedia content become more complex and the devices more diverse, the system must continue to build this universality. A central player in these efforts is Microsoft's Charles Mauzy, whose business card sports the title—take a deep breath—General Manager, Strategic Relations and Policy, Media/Entertainment and Technology Convergence Group.

Mauzy's job is to work within the various divisions of Microsoft to determine how best to integrate imaging into its overall product and corporate strategy. At the same time, he is reaching out to partners outside the company to improve the interoperability of software, devices, and communication networks in the effort to create what he and others in the industry call an *imaging ecosystem.*

Charles Mauzy

When we walked into Mauzy's office on the Microsoft campus in Redmond, Washington, the first thing we focused on were the beautiful images displayed on two 21-inch screens on his desk. In a previous career incarnation, Mauzy was an acclaimed nature photographer, and what he said about these pictures provided one of those lightbulb moments in which art, life, and technology come together: "It's amazing to me how wonderfully the notions of ecosystem and biological systems parallel business. One of the things that I always tried to do in my photography was to construct the image in such a way that, while it may look straightforward at first glance, in fact it contains an ecological message. I spent a lot of time focusing on the geology, the biology, the entire ecology depicted in those images, so that when I want to talk about temperate forests [gesturing to the image of a beautiful forest scene glowing on one of his screens], I can show you that an entire set of ecological principles is illustrated in this particular picture."

He continued, "Business ecosystems are very much the same. When you start to think about their interdependencies and interactions,

Temperate forest

you can take the same ideas and principles that I've spent years embodying in my pictures and apply them directly to business. It's the most natural kind of expression. The challenges ahead are not for one single company to solve; they're not even for just one segment of the industry to solve. This requires an entirely different approach. That's why I think in terms of this notion of an ecosystem.

"When I approach thinking about the technologies, I step back to the ultimate starting place, which is: What user experiences would I like to see enabled, and how would I like them to work? If what we're talking about is using technology to enable and expand interpersonal communication for business, let's start with the way that's most natural to us, and that's what we're doing right now: sitting together, face-to-face, having a conversation. If we're talking about how we advance our voice communication and voice-sharing technology, it should be as seamless and as painless as what we're doing right now. If we're thinking about what videoconference or chat should be like, it should be exactly like what we're doing right now.

I should have to think no more about it than just opening my mouth and talking to you. The technology I need should do more than just support that ease of communication; I'd also like to have my life organized, and accessible as a resource, in a way that mimics the situation we're in. For instance, if I want to talk about my photography or my trip to Whistler with my kids, it should be as simple as leaning over and grabbing a print and handing it to you. We're really trying to make a simple, ubiquitous set of tools so that even when we're not sitting in the same room we can enjoy the same level of clarity and simplicity of communication as if we were. There are no barriers really to what we're doing today in this room, so technology must not create barriers. That's where we run into problems today. Everybody loves the technology, but it creates barriers, so a lot of what I try to look at is how we, as an industry, can approach solving this problem."

Not surprisingly, Mauzy's peers at other key players in the *Going Visual* game have their own views. However, while these companies compete with each other in the marketplace and see the world through the lens of different corporate cultures and business objectives, we were struck by the high degree to which they are aligned on the fundamentals. Hewlett-Packard's Tara Bunch, who focuses on building a holistic, unified communication environment in her role as vice president for consumer solutions and services in the digital imaging and publishing group, told us: "If you look at today's environment, there is a lot of very cool digital gear out there, but it doesn't all talk to each other. You can't easily move images and visuals from one environment to another, and as a result, you end up with what we call 'digital islands.'

"We're seeing the emergence of a connective web that is going to move us into more of a services-based digital environment, where you can create communities on the fly, where devices can recognize one another, discover one another, rapidly share content, and essentially be functional, anywhere, anytime. In the business environment, it's driving decision making at a hyperrapid pace, with a lot less words and a lot more media as the essential content. For individuals in their personal space, that translates to 'I can share with all the people that I love and who are part of my family and social unit, and no matter where I am physically, I feel as though I'm with them. I feel like I'm there and I'm experiencing the moment.' "

Kodak's Jim Stoffel put the evolution of the ecosystem in this practical perspective: "The issue is that consumers don't want to know if something is Bluetooth or WiFi or various forms of broadband interconnect, they just want the system to work reliably. *Reliably* means, 'With my camera, whatever brand it is, I'd like to be able to walk up to a print kiosk and, whatever the equipment is inside the kiosk, push the button and get the prints.' The business solutions are going to be driven by the ecosystem, not by our favorite standard. The ecosystem will determine ease of use."

Mauzy, Bunch, and Stoffel all touched on a theme we've seen run through many of our conversations: How do we integrate all the data and media that we're accumulating daily, in our business and personal lives, in ways that make finding and using that data easy and meaningful? How can all the information we create in the course of a business day—meetings, phone calls, e-mails, reports, presentations, field visits, conceptual work, casual conversations, web searches, images, sounds—be organized in the most natural, transparent, and useful way? Viewed from that perspective, the ecosystem is ultimately about enabling technology to become an *experience-based* resource.

That is where the notion of an ecosystem—where information can flow freely across products and systems—finds its necessary complement: *smart data.* The logical link for all the day-to-day experiences we have is our own personal data trail, and the smarter we make our data, the more we can integrate it into a coherent, accessible resource.

The smart images described in our Clear Channel example provide "experience" data in the form of time, date, location, client, and product type, which connect directly to schedules, contracts, proposals, and project planning. With smart enough data, so to speak, an individual could instantly call up every asset related to a given project. The more the open standards of the ecosystem allow this information to be accessed and shared, the more powerful the individual pieces of everyday data become.

Philippe Kahn shared with us his thinking regarding the opportunities to obtain smart data from the ecosystem network that supports the most recent generation of mobile appliances: the camera phone.

"The interesting thing about camera phones," he said, "is that they know many things because of their connection to the network infrastructure. We, as an infrastructure provider, know many things about the person using the device. We have a pretty good idea where this device is; in fact, we can tell where it is within a block. We have a pretty good idea where the device has been for the last week or two; we keep a history of that. So, if a particular device finds that it is at Monster Park (formerly Candlestick Park, the home stadium of the San Francisco 49ers professional football team), and it knows that sports are played there, and it's probably football, it can look on the system's server and see the schedule, so it knows who's playing. When you take a picture and send it from there, a lot of metadata, information about the picture, can be attached to it automatically: the date, time, location, possibly the fact that the 49ers beat the Raiders in that game. This picture can be very intelligently annotated, and a lot of links can be created about this event. Suddenly, you have a much more interesting story than is being told by just going click, all done automatically. The more you help people create a rich environment automatically in this area of personal-content creation, the more interesting it gets and the more valuable these devices get."

Kahn continued, "There is a lot of information that comes from the fact that these devices are always connected. They know where they are; they know what's around them; and they have a pretty good idea of what you're doing. They know where you work every day, so they know that a picture taken at that location is a work picture. They would know, by looking at your calendar, that that picture was taken at the sales luncheon to celebrate the Salesman of the Year. So that picture, shared through the office, gets an interesting annotation.

"A lot can happen by relating information about time and location to a picture. We all have calendars, and matching the time and location on our calendars allows us to derive tons of information. It's part of all the processes in your life becoming mobile, becoming digital, and having all this intelligence. That applies both in the enterprise and in your personal life. All of this helps the picture become instantly smart. In the future, we'll also be able to apply pattern recognition to the images, which will analyze things like colors and shapes, and we'll have a very smart system that does a lot of things automatically for people. This will mean a radical simplification of the user experience as well as exciting new possibilities to make people more efficient and more creative."

Any of the images described in this book could benefit by creating smart personal content. Hyder & Company's field photos could automatically be tied to a time, date, location, project, and individual. Sally Carrocino could easily keep track of which image was taken at which client stop. The home and garden images taken around the world by HomeGo reps would have automatic references to the country, the industry show, or even the street in Rome where an image was taken, and which representative or designer took it. Clear Channel could eliminate its manual input of the basic time, location, and project information and have those details attached to the image automatically. This "experience" data merges image and text into a powerful new form of information linked directly to our everyday lives.

VISUAL MOBILITY AND THE THIRD SCREEN

Mobile visual communication, manifested in the camera phone, represents one of the most striking examples of the trend toward creating a kind of personalized technology that is accessible anywhere and anytime such that it fits the circumstances of our lives.

When considering what can only be adequately described as the camera-phone phenomenon—the device exploded on the global stage in 2001 with such force that by 2004 it outsold all other forms of cameras (film and digital) combined—we're powerfully reminded of a phrase we heard many times during our travels: "This is something that *wants* to happen." This was spoken by technologists, inventors, artists, and educators to describe technology developments that have been part of our consciousness for as long as we've been dreaming of the future.

The camera phone, an intelligent personal tool that includes communication, information, and imaging capabilities, has "wanted to happen" for decades. As impressive as today's models are, they're just the tip of the iceberg. A device that can fulfill the basic dream of the "personal communicator" has now emerged in the marketplace . . . and the broadening of its capabilities begins. (In this regard, we fully expect that, for many of our readers, the very mention of the camera phone and its power to transform communication will generate controversy. Examples of misuse of the technology, as well as some of its very best uses, have been featured prominently in the mass media. In fact, the implications of an imaging device we have with us at all times, one that is permanently connected to the global network, are profound. They go well beyond the realm of business and extend into our social, cultural, and political worlds—and ultimately, perhaps, into our very physiology. For that reason, we return to this point in the afterword of this book.)

Although camera phones have been available worldwide only since 2001, and in the United States since 2003, they have been improved and enhanced more aggressively than any consumer product in history. In 2003, most cell phone screens were black and white; now color screens are the rule, and the quality of those screens is often startlingly good. The screens are designed to display the same kind of content we're used to seeing on our computers and TVs. As more of us use our phones for viewing e-mail and images, web browsing, appointment calendars, and contact information, they become central to our personal and work lifestyles and, after our TV and computer, are emerging as the third screen in our lives.

The transition from cameras to camera phones parallels the history of the telephone. Before the introduction of the mobile phone, voice communication was limited to wired phones in homes and offices, or in public places via pay phones—in other words, physical access to the wires enabled communication. Wireless communications changed the rules forever, making an anytime, virtually anywhere connection a reality and freeing us to stay in touch without having to stay in place.

Similarly, while the digitization of imaging was the first step in untethering pictures from paper printouts, a physical connection to a wired access point was still necessary in order for images to travel over networks. Now that the image-capturing devices themselves are equipped to wirelessly send and receive images, anytime, anywhere, visual communication will become as natural a part of our behavior as voice conversations.

Adel Al-Saleh, who is responsible for the business, applications, and solutions-related aspects of IBM's wireless and mobile initiatives around the world, spoke about the implications of this evolution of wireless, always-on communications with respect to the conduct of daily business: "What's changing dramatically is the whole notion of extending e-business into wireless environments, how you run your business on the web using completely new devices. Whether it's motivated by economic conditions or by competition or both, businesses are trying to innovate in their processes in order to become more efficient. What's so compelling about wireless is that no matter where you are in the organization—whether you're in manufacturing or marketing or development or distribution, it doesn't really matter—what wireless allows you to do is, first of all, capture the information when it is created, at the point of creation, and then deliver it, real time, to the right people so they can make the right decisions and make them fast. We call this 'real-time business,' and it's very compelling in today's environment."

For all the reasons we've discussed, getting the right information to the right people at the right time is even more powerful when that information is visual. That's where camera phones play a crucial role, not just as a way of capturing images and video, but also—at the other end of the communication—as a way of viewing them.

In our Hyder, HomeGo, and Clear Channel models, the efficiencies of mobile imaging would improve business operations by streamlining the linking of images to the relevant documents that drive the decision-making process. Adobe's Bryan Lamkin observed, "Think of how people are using images in mobile situations. They are going out to inspect a building, going out to inspect a car, going out to write a report on their competitor's offerings at retail. Those are situations where there is very rich potential for new forms of integration between documents and forms, on the one hand, and images on the other. A form is a document that enables a decision.

We're focused on making it much easier to accelerate business processes and decision processes around documents. I can envision that we'll be able to have some of the more standardized imaging work flows routinely operated from within intelligent forms. For example, if I'm a building inspector and I'm approving a stage in a construction project, I take a picture of it, upload it from my mobile device, and the server-based process automatically circulates the image along with the approval form. Images and video will play a critical role in accompanying form-based processes."

The streamlining of the forms process would have the following positive effects on Hyder's field reports describing maintenance projects, HomeGo's retail managers' reports on sales displays, or Clear Channel's proof-of-performance reports:

- A report would take less time to create through an automated process.

- A report would be more accurate because the visual and text information would be linked through a smart image and a document database.

- A report would be delivered faster to the Community of Interest because the device on which it was created would be connected wirelessly to the network.

As of this writing, *visual conversations,* meaning conversations that are carried out in significant part through a back-and-forth exchange of still images (or short videos) between two people using camera phones, are made difficult by a number of technical factors. However, Phil Garrison, who oversees the development of Sprint's wireless devices, told us that "the [telecommunications] industry is pushing very hard to achieve global intercarrier operability [meaning that all types of information can be exchanged from one carrier

to another, for example, from Sprint to AT&T] across all networks, regardless of whether they are high-bandwidth, low-bandwidth, fixed, or mobile, so it all works everywhere there's a constant connection, and that also includes cable and broadband access. I would say it's more than imminent. It's well on its way toward completion."

Once again, the key to this transformation is the evolution of the camera phone into a device most of us have, or will have, with us during all our waking hours. In the next few years, as executives from the information-processing and telecommunications industries work to bridge their two worlds, camera phones will become fully integrated, as information-sending and -receiving devices, into the networks of corporate resources such as the one we described in Chapter 6, "Smart Images." Documents, images, videos, archive services, directories—all the elements of distributed computing systems—will be accessible anytime, anywhere on these handheld devices.

We expect the process to be quite rapid, given that the lessons learned during the maturation of distributed computing will be applied to distributed imaging using many of the same core technologies, database, wireless infrastructure, user interface design, and rights management. For the most part, there is no need to develop new technologies, only the specific solutions that meet particular customer needs.

THE MANY SCREENS IN OUR LIVES

Over the next few years, as more information goes visual, many innovative ways of displaying images will emerge. We turned to Microsoft's chief technology officer, Craig Mundie, whose vision helps drive his company's research and development in this area, to reveal the horizon of possibilities.

"The way we think about it," Mundie said, "is that there are actually going to be lots of screens in your life, and how you interact with them should be limited only by the fact that these screens will vary in size. In all other ways, it should be as scalable and uniform as possible. We think that the smallest screens in your life will be jewelry, like watches, and the next biggest screen in your life will be what we call your *communicator.* Broadly defined, communicators now exist in two basic flavors, which we call the *one-hand form factor* and the *two-hand form factor.* A one-hand communicator is basically a small screen with no keyboard; the whole mode of operation is 'look at and talk' and 'hold and manipulate' in a single hand. The PDA/phone combination is a superset of that. It's a two-hand device on which you can annotate by using a keyboard to type with your thumbs or fingers, or by using the screen as a pad to write with a stylus or a fingernail. When you make that transition from one to two

One-hand camera phone   Two-hand smart camera phone

hands, you move from a 'display and verbal comment' (or 'display and no comment') environment to a 'see what I mean' environment where you can interact with the content.

"Think about the screens on your household appliances," Mundie continued. "They're much smaller than those on a device that would be used for a desktop or an entertainment presentation. Think of a display on the dashboard of your car. There are a great many devices we use in our everyday lives that could in the future include displays, and the information on those displays is communicated almost 100 percent by glancing at an image, as opposed to reading text.

"We've showed a concept demonstration of a personalized alarm clock, and that was essentially an image-based display. Of course, your clock today, if it has hands rather than numerals, is already an image-based way of communicating time, but what we wanted to show is that, if you think of a clock more generally as being your bedside graphic display, then in addition to showing you the time it can also show you the weather, have your favorite stock with a big green or red arrow next to it—you know, all these things that we do visually today, but that we don't do in all the places where it could be useful. So, do I think your phone will be the third screen? Yes, or maybe it will be the fourth or fifth screen. Perhaps it'll be the second screen. That sequence is ultimately not important, but what is important, and very much so, is deciding on a consistent way of presenting classes of information by visual representation on the appropriate displays at the appropriate time."

AUTOMATIC IMAGING

Whether by security cameras, personal webcams, or reconnaissance satellites, images that are potentially relevant to our society are being captured continuously, and in exponentially larger numbers every day, by a dramatically growing population of devices. Some of these devices in our homes and businesses are under our individual control, while many, controlled by corporations, institutions, governments, and municipalities, are not. These always-on, unattended, network-connected imaging devices are the tools of the phenomenon we refer to as *automatic imaging*.

The ever-increasing need to ensure safety in our society is driving the use of security cameras in facilities, on city streets, and orbiting in space. That presents us with an unprecedented set of societal challenges, as well as business opportunities. In our afterword, we touch on the important issues of privacy and access to information that are raised by automatic imaging. In this chapter, our focus is on some of the business opportunities created by the automatic gathering of visual information. The number and quality of image data being captured automatically for both government and private use have become so vast, and the means of distribution—the Internet—so universally accessible, that the opportunities to use this content for multiple purposes, regardless of the reasons for which it was originally gathered, are too enticing to ignore.

Jim Stoffel talked to us in his Rochester, New York, office about his evolving interest in the value of satellite imagery to businesses. Stoffel oversees Kodak's research and development efforts, including its large staff of in-house scientists, as well as its relationships with outside companies working on technologies that Kodak might find of interest. In a nutshell, he's the imaging giant's technology czar. His comments illustrate a profound and positive unintended consequence of an elaborate imaging system that was originally built for security purposes, but that has now found a new market wherein it provides visual information for everyday business applications.

"I think passive, or automatic, imaging is going to become more and more useful," Stoffel said. "You know, we have these satellites taking pictures all the time. It's been a constant over the past 20 years that if you looked at the Earth Resources Technology Satellite [ERTS] data, you'd realize, boy, they do take good pictures—I can see the crop of corn that went bad in Africa. There's so much data here, how do we make it useful, and how do we get it to the people who can benefit from it? That process of making visual data useful and accessible is beginning to happen, in part due to developments in all the other elements in the imaging chain: You'll have greater processing power and cheaper, decentralized storage, not just at NSA [National Security Agency] in Washington but available to a lot of people. For example, we have a web service that we use for a variety of applications, one of which is to provide an easy way to keep track of the condition of all the golf courses across Florida. We've been scanning golf courses to tell their operators when they need watering. We have another service that's very real and practical, which looks for leaks in pipes—water, sewage, oil, and so on. We also do other projects, like placement of satellite towers for cell phones."

Golf course satellite image

Boulder, Colorado, satellite image

We asked Jim about the use of satellite imagery of cities. We had seen visual mapping projects of urban areas such as Cambridge, Massachusetts, at MIT, and Westwood, California, at UCLA, and wondered how information gathered on the ground might be integrated with images captured from space. "We have software now where we scan across a city and give you the 3D view of that city, so you can see the height and location information that pertains to a city scene and 'fly around' it. We offer this service today for 30 cities."

Stoffel sees these ventures as only the beginning of meaningful business access to automatic images: "I certainly expect satellite imagery at less than a meter resolution [meaning objects measuring less than a meter will be recognizable in the images] will become available off the web [the electronic equivalent of off the shelf]. Today, I see satellite images every 15 minutes. I just ping my favorite weather channel, and it runs a little movie for me. My system is on all day, so whenever I'm home in Rochester, it's become a habit to check on the changing weather conditions. Capture is ubiquitous, by satellites all over the world."

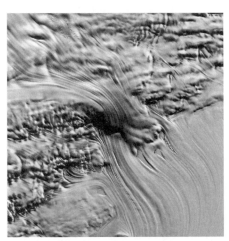 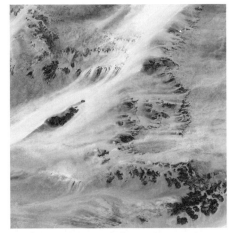

These two images captured by Landsat demonstrate that visual information can be not only useful, but also beautiful

As exciting as the possibilities are for business use of satellite imagery, there is much more to automatic imaging, as the population of cameras capable of delivering automatic image streams is growing here on earth even faster than it is in space.

Stoffel brought the examples down to earth, "I do think that there will be an explosion of the personal use of webcams because now you can get a webcam acting as its own server; it can have its own IP address, so consumers can set up cameras, connect them to their cable TV Internet portal, and keep track of their homes [or businesses] themselves. A friend of mine in Florida had one set up so he could check on his home and see if a storm hit, and did he have anything left? It is down at the consumer level today, so we're going to see more and more of that kind of thing."

On another automatic imaging front, it's been said that one can't travel more than a few hundred feet anywhere in London without encountering a surveillance camera, that a full-length feature film could be made of any individual's travels through that city during a single day based solely on collecting and aggregating footage from surveillance cameras. These observations testify to the evolution of visual surveillance in a city that has been coping with violent political terrorism for decades. In what is becoming known as the "post-9/11 era" (significantly, the only images of the plane crashing into the Pentagon that day were captured by a security camera), much of the West is becoming "Londonized," but with the benefit of more modern technology. We fully expect that this unhappy set of circumstances will eventually yield some highly positive unintended consequences. After all, the Internet, too, was originally developed for military use: Its purpose was to ensure the survival of control and command capabilities if major U.S. computing centers were destroyed in a nuclear attack.

To get a sense of the possible, consider the value to emergency services—private as well as public—of having access to the visual information generated by the surveillance grid. It could be as simple as getting real-time updates on traffic congestion to map the most efficient route to an accident site; or, in a more sophisticated application, emergency police or fire rescue units could combine surveillance images with 3D maps of the streets and buildings they were about to encounter, such as those discussed by Jim Stoffel, to obtain a virtual model of the location they are heading to even before they reach it. Imagine how services of this type could have assisted rescue efforts in the Twin Towers, or how many lives might have been saved had rescuers been privy to images of the condition of the various stairwells provided by surveillance cameras connected to a network accessible via the Internet.

VIVID IMAGING

Jim Stoffel's example of using satellite images to build 3D models of cities provides a natural link to our fourth topic: *vivid imaging.* As wonderful as photography is, we tend to forget that it renders only a very small fraction of the totality of our visual experience. It captures the small slice of our field of vision that's seen through a lens, and it does so in a momentary slice of time—the fraction of a second when the shutter clicks. It then reproduces that information in only two dimensions, length and width, while flattening a third dimension, depth. The term *vivid imaging* is our shorthand for the notion that what we're striving for is the ability to reproduce our entire visual experience, and that experience includes continuity of time, a broad field of view, and the full three dimensions that we perceive.

One subtle but significant element in the evolution of imaging devices is the merging of still- and video-capture capabilities. In the early 1990s, digital cameras mimicked traditional still-film cameras and captured frozen moments of time. Beginning in the late 1990s, video capability began to appear in digital cameras in the form of short bursts, generally 5 to 60 seconds, of video capture. This type of video-capture capability, now available in most digital cameras, is rapidly being deployed in camera phones. We call these bursts of video a *long picture*. The advantage of the long picture is that it extends the traditional photographic moment from a fraction of a second to tens of seconds, or minutes, while retaining the simple, manageable file structure associated with single images. While they can be edited, long pictures can also be shot with the purpose of capturing a short, continuous action.

Pedro Meyer, an internationally acclaimed photographer and essayist, whose ZoneZero web site exhibits photography and video from around the world, believes long pictures have great potential: "These short movies change the nature of communication because they are not video, but not still images, either. This is a new medium, which has a new delivery mechanism. When I tell people that we had an entire festival in Mexico of one-minute films, they find that very surprising. But why is this surprising? You have 30-second commercials and nobody thinks of them as anything special, and how much money is invested in 30-second commercials? This is a vehicle to communicate, the one-minute film."

Whether lasting one minute or 10 seconds, the long picture is a simple but profoundly effective communication tool that is beginning to find numerous uses in business whenever some length of time is required for the image to communicate its information. Many activities can be effectively captured in short bursts of video and put to use in training, sales, maintenance, and emergency applications, such as showing how to demonstrate a product, how two parts fit together, how to correctly operate a simple device, or how to open a security door. The straightforward, concise nature of this format makes it possible to use as a rich, direct communication medium.

Another way that vivid imaging is emerging in business applications is in the 360-degree viewing of houses in the real estate industry, hotel rooms in the travel industry, and car interiors in the automotive industry. The next dimension in viewing technology is the arrival of the most enduring "what wants to happen" visual concept—stereo 3D.

We traveled to the Santa Monica, California, headquarters of Dynamic Digital Depth (DDD), which is developing software to produce stereo 3D images that can be viewed without special glasses. There we spoke with CEO Chris Yewdall, who began his comments with a fundamental idea: "There's a reason that we need two eyes. It's so that we can perceive depth and interact with objects at close quarters. Over a period of time, we haven't evolved down to one eye, as we would have if the world were a two-dimensional place. It's actually a three-dimensional place, and our perception of depth is very important. We know that if you can make an image look more lifelike and realistic, more in keeping with what we're expecting to see when we're walking around in the real world, viewers will absorb it much more readily.

"Because we're absorbing the world in 3D," Yewdall explained, "in our visual memory our brain is actually recording depth cues of what we look at, so you tend to have a much easier time remembering an experience of being physically somewhere, because you're able to absorb the dimensional aspect of it. There's a very simple fact here: If you present the depth cues in the content in the way that we'd expect to see it if we were physically there, our brain absorbs those depth cues and it gives us a stronger ability to recall what we've seen subsequent to the event.

"This has great value at a number of levels. If you're a business whose job it is to get your message and brand out in front of a target customer, then the ability to present it in 3D, and know that the customers are going to remember what you showed them when they walk away from it, is incredibly valuable. To give you an example, we put a 3D plasma screen in a music store here in Los Angeles. We showed music videos and DVD film trailers for feature films in 3D, right in the middle of a bunch of regular 2D screens running pretty much the same material. We exit-polled around 200 people coming out of the store, and we asked them whether they saw anything different. Typically about the same number of people noticed the 3D screen as noticed the 2D screens. There was only one 3D and 20 or so 2Ds, but when you asked them if they watched the 3D screen, and what did they see on it, 72 percent of them could remember exactly what they saw. 'Yeah, I saw Shrek, I saw Madonna, the Dave Matthews Band'—whatever it was on the screen, they could tell you. When you asked them what they saw on the 2D screens, there was less than 10 percent recall. That's what I call a very powerful tool."

James Stephens, a scientist working at Eastman Kodak's System Concepts Center, where much of the company's research on advanced user concepts takes place, made an equally compelling case for the power of stereo 3D: "What we're after is the creation of an experience that's as good or better than being in the place that the imagery depicts. We also want to recognize in our plans that once you create these rich, immersive environments for people to go into, the next thing that they are going to want to do is navigate their own way through those spaces. We want to go from passive to interactive experiences within these virtual worlds that are photographic in nature. We want to bring down the cost of these things to where, ultimately, we may be able to replace the monitor that's on your desktop or the television in your living room.

"What does it take for a human being to really feel present in an environment rather than feel that they're looking at a picture?" Stephens asked. "What does understanding that then imply about the nature of the imaging environment that you need to create? We need to engage a much wider segment of the observer's field of view. We know that, depending on the individual, somewhere within 60 to 80 degrees—certainly by the time you have a 90-degree field of view—people go from the sense of looking at a picture to a sense of being in the scene."

Stephens described a broad array of potential 3D application: "We start at the high end with military training and simulation, then focus on location-based entertainment experiences at places like theme parks, and work down to family arcades in the mall. Then we're developing workstations where you can do design, engineering, education, and health. We have a very long list, including photo-realistic experiences that are meant to transport you to a different place. The findings on the value of immersive environments for comprehension and retention of information are striking. In the medical arena, the University of Washington did studies in which they took burn patients who have to go through excruciating treatments, and found that if you could engage them in these immersive worlds, it so captivated their cognitive attention that the pain-medicine levels dramatically decreased. In the antiterrorism realm, we envision viewing stations with fast scanning and reviewing capabilities that will allow airport screeners to see information about what is inside luggage in 3D, so they'll be better able to spot potentially dangerous objects. Of course, the next step is to add some smart capabilities that recognize certain objects and highlight them for the screeners as they go by."

John McIntosh, chairman of the Computer Art Department at the School of Visual Arts in New York City, looks at 3D from the perspective of working with the next generation of image makers. "With respect to visual literacy we have to think in terms of becoming 3D-literate, not just 2D-literate. That's what the next generation is interested in. They don't live in a 2D world; they live in a 3D world. How does a still image, or a sequence of images, give more information more effectively? By using that simple spatial information to which we've become accustomed to generate another layer of information about the scene. It's not just about aesthetics, it's about the fact that technology enables us to process these images in more sophisticated ways. As a result, we will be able to extrapolate more information than we get from the current 2D surface reality that is affected by light and tone and contrast."

McIntosh continues, "For instance, what if you could take two images of an office from two different perspectives and extrapolate from that all the depth information so that you could get accurate measurements—possibly within millimeters—of the entire office? Would that be more valuable than an old-fashioned 2D image? Absolutely. With 3D I can give you more information so that a picture of the room doesn't just 'look big'—I can inform you that the room actually measures 40 feet by 60 feet. You can extrapolate that information directly from the images, and then you can place image objects in the virtual space. Say, for example, you have an image of a nine-foot couch, or a six-foot desk, or a conference table—all of these images become very useful 3D information that solves real problems."

McIntosh expanded the conversation from still to video images, "If video footage were 3D, you would have the functional ability to look in different directions. You would be able to go from a view of the main subject in a scene to looking around elsewhere to see what else was taking place. When you change your viewing perspective, you get new information. Being able to choose the viewing perspective allows the viewer to say, 'Whose perspective am I looking at here?' and ultimately, 'Whose perspective am I adopting?' The idea isn't that seeing the scene from behind or from the side necessarily changes what I see in that scene, but that it gives me a greater sense of proximity, of intimacy to an event—and that's what I'm looking for. It's very powerful. It's a human need for things to be seen in more than two dimensions. As a way to record and archive information, 3D has immense value."

PERSONALIZED AUTHORING

Stephens's point about helping security inspectors examine the contents of luggage, mundane as it may appear, goes to the heart of our fifth issue. There is a powerful paradox in imaging: While the ability to produce still and motion images is exploding, our ability to view them is limited by resources that are *not* expanding: our own time and our ability to concentrate. The baggage inspector is faced with hundreds of thousands of images during his or her shift, all displaying the insides of luggage. Here's someone who needs help. Similarly, in the video realm, where the capturing of hours of footage is typical, the greatest barrier to easy, everyday use is the process of editing the content into a coherent, interesting, and effective presentation.

Making images or short bursts of video smarter, as described earlier, goes a long way toward helping to organize them, and desktop video-editing tools have advanced significantly in recent years insofar as their cost and ease of use, but the time and effort required to use them are still on the high side of the curve for most business-people. Help is on the way in the form of personalized authoring software that will automate the editing process and democratize video to the point where it will become an everyday business tool. The challenge of the usability of raw content is being met by the development of intelligent systems that can organize content on the fly to suit the needs of specific viewers and authors.

The principle behind personalized authoring is that if you start with hours of video, different parts of that video tell different stories that are relevant to different viewers. Two hours of video footage of a trade show may have valuable images of competitive products, booth displays, marketing materials, technical demonstrations, even conversations with industry experts. It is unlikely that many in the organization would, or should, sit through the entire two hours; the real value is matching the content with the audience. Personalized authoring promises the ability to set some parameters and produce a custom-edited presentation in the form of, say, a 2½-minute quick overview or a 10-minute detailed movie that provides a specific audience with the precise information it is interested in. The concepts presented next are critical components in democratizing the creation of effective, engaging, usable video content.

Professor Michael Bove of the MIT Media Lab put the science of personalized authoring beautifully: "The notion that you have this video that knows what's in it is somewhat magical. The idea is: How do we make a video that plays out differently under different circumstances or for different viewers? We created a video-editing environment that lets me say, 'Here are a bunch of possible variables about a viewer that will be known at the moment of viewing.' Then I can give the system a set of rules for how to tell stories under different circumstances. If you're a small screen, do this; if you're a big screen, do this. If you're in this neighborhood, do this. If you've seen this before, do this. If you're in a hurry, do this.'

"I can, when I edit a clip," Bove explained, "say, okay, there's a critical part that you have to see, but if you have more time, you can cut in anywhere and it's visually acceptable, and you can cut out anywhere, so we can make a video that is self-summarizing. Hit the fast-forward button and you see this part. So we have one set of variables about the content, and we have another set of variables about the viewer.

"Here's an example: A student who works with my colleague Glorianna Davenport was running for a graduate-school student council governmental office. We did a campaign commercial for her.

Her constituency was students who work in the Media Lab, so based on what floor of the building you work on, it shows her spending more time in your neighborhood, and, based on what e-mail list you subscribe to, it shows her talking about those appropriate topics. If you're in a hurry, the edit decision list can collapse down, so what you see is a perfectly acceptable edit that just happens to be very tight. Certain scenes have dropped out, and you have alternative shots in some cases. This is the solution to the TiVo problem, where you come home and you've got six hours of video and you've got two hours to watch it.

"The important thing that's going on here is something really radical," Bove continued. "You're not doing the edit until the viewer sees it. You're creating this document that reacts to facts about you and your viewing circumstances and your history right now and turns that into video. The problem has been that there have been no tools to let someone who is a visual thinker create that. So that's what this is about—the video has a sense of what's in it."

Building software that automatically examines the visual data itself to make the presentation smart is another way of considering personalized authoring. By analyzing image properties such as color, light levels, shapes, movement, and changes in the scene, so much can be learned about the images and their relation to one another that a cohesive story can be assembled.

Microsoft's Craig Mundie described this authoring approach: "In the very near future, you'll be able to take a movie of your business trip. Let's say you have an hour's worth of video, and when you come back you feed it into the computer and you say, 'I'd like a two-and-a-half-minute executive summary of my trip, please. Here's all the raw video.' The software will actually analyze the raw video and figure out where the scene changes by looking for fundamentally different images, what was the relative importance of these based on the total amount of raw footage, and so on. Then it does all of the panning and zooming and adds a score, and out pops a two-and-a-half-minute movie. That's the kind of thing that I think, either for business or personal communication, particularly in the video domain, makes this stuff a lot more usable, because otherwise movies made by average people, whether for business or personal reasons, are pretty much unusable. I saw a demo of some of our research work recently where 30 minutes of video produced a two-minute movie, including adding the score and the cinematography effects in a matter of seconds. That does give essentially on-demand, personalized video capability."

Over the next three years, the evolution of the imaging ecosystem will provide those who are *Going Visual* with increasingly richer, more useful tools that are seamlessly integrated into their lives. Images are going to be as commonplace in our personal and professional lives as e-mail has become today. We're going to be working in a multimedia world and trying to remember what a single-media world was all about.

Afterword: New Challenges Ahead

In the preceding pages, we've explored the historic opportunity that businesses large and small have today to harness a historic change in the tool set of communication and, by doing so, to become more productive, efficient, and profitable—in a word, more competitive. In this book, that has been our singular purpose.

We do, however, feel a responsibility to acknowledge that the issues raised by the emergence of visual communication as a mainstream application have vastly broader ramifications than merely offering the opportunity for businesses to become more competitive. The following is our contribution to what we hope will be a thoughtful debate of these broader social and political implications.

In our section on automatic imaging, we touched on the explosive growth in the numbers of observation and surveillance cameras being put into operation, both in space and on the ground. For a dramatic illustration, we quote a *New York Times* article of September 21, 2004, reporting on the planned installation of 250 new surveillance cameras by the City of Chicago:

A highly advanced system of video surveillance that Chicago officials plan to install by 2006 will make people here some of the most closely observed in the world. Mayor Richard M. Daley says it will also make them much safer. "Cameras are the equivalent of hundreds of sets of eyes," Mr. Daley said when he unveiled the new project this month. "They're the next best thing to having police officers stationed at every potential trouble spot." Police specialists here can already monitor live footage from about 2,000 surveillance cameras around the city, so the addition of 250 cameras under the mayor's new plan is not a great jump. The way these cameras will be used, however, is an extraordinary technological leap. Sophisticated new computer programs will immediately alert the police whenever anyone viewed by any of the cameras placed at buildings and other structures considered terrorist targets wanders aimlessly in circles, lingers outside a public building, pulls a car onto the shoulder of a highway, or leaves a package and walks away from it. Images of those people will be highlighted in color at the city's central monitoring station, allowing dispatchers to send police officers to the scene immediately.

We are certainly not the first to notice, or to point out, the potential risks of widespread optical surveillance with respect to individual privacy and civil liberties. The notion that Big Brother is watching has raised concern along these lines for more than half a century. The difference is that today, in Mayor Daley's words, Big Brother has more than 2,000 eyes to watch us in Chicago alone. That is not, intrinsically, a bad thing. People certainly want to be protected against terrorism and street crime, and visual surveillance systems are a powerful tool for doing so. But the very existence of such powerful tools, and the delegation of their control to political authorities, requires of us all a high degree of civic awareness.

By the same token, we're hardly the first to point out that issues exist at the other end of the spectrum—the dark side of the democratization of visual technology and pervasive visual communication. In the world of business, the issues raised typically relate to protecting intellectual property, process advantage, or first-to-know advantage. As our garden retailer, Michelle Kline, put it: "We go to trade shows where people come from many different countries to show their wares. And because we're all out there trying to get the newest, greatest idea from someone else, these trade shows have huge signs that say 'No cameras.' They have show police everywhere making sure, and if they catch you, they will physically take your camera away because they want you to understand that it's that serious. Now that there are phones that have cameras built-in, it's made things much more complicated, and everyone is even more nervous."

The abusive capture and use of images for industrial espionage, voyeurism, identity theft, witness intimidation, exam cheating, and all manner of privacy invasion is already getting much play in the media. It sells papers, and it provides politicians with always-welcome opportunities for righteous indignation. Which is not to say that these abuses are benign—quite the contrary; this is an issue to be taken seriously. One could argue that unobtrusive spy cameras have existed for decades. They were not, however, produced in the hundreds of millions, handed to virtually everyone, or connected to a worldwide network that enables their images to be viewed instantly by anyone, anywhere.

It is only reasonable, therefore, for companies to mandate that visitors leave their camera phones at the reception desk, for health clubs to prohibit them in locker rooms, for officials to forbid them in courtrooms to protect undercover officers, and so on. It's also only to be expected, unfortunately, that broadly restrictive legislation will be proposed in the spirit of scoring political points rather than in a manner that addresses the issues in a truly constructive fashion.

Doing so requires, first of all, understanding that there will be no returning to the circumstances of the twentieth century, where the vast majority of visual information was produced and distributed exclusively by the media, and the rules regarding who could see what, and under what circumstances, resulted from agreements, formal or informal, between those controlling the media and those controlling the government. The Internet and digital imaging have fostered modes of creation and distribution of visual information to which these old rules don't apply, and to which they can't be applied. The U.S. military learned as much with the Iraq Abu Ghraib prison scandal, as evidenced by Secretary of Defense Donald Rumsfeld's testimony in front of the U.S. House of Representatives Armed Services Committee on May 7, 2004: "We are constantly finding that we have procedures and habits that have evolved over the years from the last century that don't really fit the 21st century. They don't fit the Information Age. They don't fit a time when people are running around with digital cameras."

A society in which all or even a majority of its citizens become empowered to communicate visually, having with them at all times an image-capturing device that is connected to the global communications network, is bound to experience new forms of interaction that in turn are likely to drive significant social and political changes. Take, for instance, the phenomenon known as *photoblogs*, a dynamic form of visual, online journals. Photoblogs are designed to be updated frequently simply by sending images and text to an online site that has capabilities for viewer comments and linkage to other sites. These photoblogs greatly extend the reach of visual communication by making images available in a public forum to anyone in the world with an Internet connection. The fastest-growing types of photoblogs are those whose images come directly from camera phones; these have been dubbed *moblogs,* short for "mobile blogs." Most of the images currently on these moblogs are personal, but, like everything else in *Going Visual,* the boundaries between the personal, professional, and societal use of images intermingle.

Hewlett-Packard is one of many businesses looking at moblogs with great interest, and the company's Phil McKinney told us he views them as a potentially important source of a new kind of information, "an area that we've been focusing on fairly heavily in our research we call 'social reporting.' We're focusing on camera phones, working on making it very simple for someone to snap a picture and post it. One button to take the picture, and with one more click it self-publishes right to the photoblog. But we also want to automatically capture as much information as possible about the experience of taking the picture, and publish that along with the image. So you can do voice annotation. You get the date and time, the latitude and longitude of where you're standing when you snap that picture; we publish all that on the blog. Our research team uses a map to geoposition where the photographs are being taken. You can watch the photoblog, and as photos are taken, little dots appear on the map.

"One day we saw a burst of photographs occurring in San Jose, California. It wasn't just one—it was a whole lot of photographs appearing all of a sudden, and we thought, 'Something has got to be going on over there. What is it?' When we clicked on the photographs, we saw there was a huge building fire in San Jose. Someone had whipped out their phone and was snapping a bunch of pictures and posting them to the blog. So I'm based in Washington, D.C., and from there I can see a building fire in San Jose, probably before the local emergency services are even aware of it. If you look at it from the standpoint of an emergency responder, you could receive photographs from a location where something was happening, nearly in real time, without having to deploy somebody to go there to take them."

For a stark but powerful example of how this change in technology and the corresponding change in behavior might affect all of us, and possibly change the course of future human events, consider the terrorist attacks of September 11, 2001. The fact that the events of that day are the most photographed and videotaped in history attests to the pervasiveness and democratization of image capturing already achieved in our society. Many of the iconic images of the attacks on the World Trade Center and the Pentagon were captured not by professional press photographers, but by everyday people who happened to be in the area carrying video or still-image cameras and who spontaneously recorded the epic scenes as they unfolded. Some historic scenes, such as the attack on the Pentagon, were recorded only by unattended security cameras.

We'll leave it to others to comment on editorial decisions that news organizations made regarding what images were suitable to show to their audiences. With all the coverage, however, there are critical images of the events of that day that we will never see, images that were not captured or, if captured, were trapped inside the buildings or the planes and were destroyed along with them. We saw no images from inside the World Trade Center after the planes struck, no images of the mixture of chaos and calm that must have prevailed in the 18 minutes between the strike at Tower One and the crash at Tower Two. What did the people inside the buildings see? Would a picture have immediately revealed the deadly plane was an airliner, not a small private plane as was first suspected? Would pictures from inside the towers have given police and fire officials valuable information about the conditions they were blindly trying to control? Would the last phone call to a loved one have included a last look, a last moment of profound connection? Likewise, on the four hijacked planes, numerous cell phone calls were made to coworkers and loved ones reporting a terrorist takeover, but, except for a snippet of video recovered later from the wreckage of United Flight 93 in a Pennsylvania field, no images of the takeovers exist.

If these terrible events were to take place today, only a few years later, in all probability there would be people on the planes and in the towers with camera phones. We can only guess about the effect an image snapped and transmitted in the first stages of one of the airplane hijackings might have had on the events of 9/11. Perhaps a picture of the hostage taking in progress sent from a camera phone, alerting airline and government agencies to the unfolding horror, might have made a difference. Perhaps pictures from inside the towers, showing the condition of the various stairwells and hallways, would have saved the lives of both rescuers and victims.

The greatest challenge we face is balancing the positive and negative effects that the power of new imaging technologies and techniques will have on society. The issue of security, of who has access to what images, will be central to any discussion of the future of *Going Visual.*

In many ways our relationship to technology is akin to that of laborers working on a small portion of a vast construction project whose overall plan is not available to them. We can only interpret what we're doing in light of what we've done before, and no more than dimly glimpse the place our own footsteps lead us to. This is why works of science fiction are so often revealed, with hindsight, to be less predictions of the future than reflections of their own time.

We'd be foolish to claim we have the answers to the big questions we've raised here. Rather, our goal is that, as you begin your *Going Visual* journey, you have in the back of your mind some of these broader issues. It's our hope that, as all of us welcome this new mode of communication, our growing sophistication will shape ideas and opinions that will, in time, be brought to bear on these issues, so that embracing technology will prove to have made us not only better businesspeople, but also better citizens.

www.GoingVisual.com

This book, *Going Visual,* is just a starting point for those of us investigating the power of images to improve communication. The journey continues at www.goingvisual.com, where you can share and learn from the experiences of other businesses, large and small, that are *Going Visual* too. Find out what has worked for them that might also work for you, what pitfalls to avoid, and what innovative ideas are worth a try. Tell us, and tell them, how the ideas and examples in this book have helped you improve your business. At GoingVisual.com you will also find the latest information about imaging products that can improve your business—digital cameras, camera phones, camcorders, PCs, and printers, as well as software for imaging, imaging presentation, editing, management, security, and enterprise networking—all the technology pieces necessary to Go Visual. GoingVisual.com will also provide information specifically relevant to particular industry sectors, such as construction, medical, manufacturing, retails sales, travel, real estate, and insurance. The "lightbulb moments" continue on GoingVisual.com. Please join us there.

Appendix: Insiders' Views of the Mobile Imaging Industry

W ithout a doubt, the most dynamic area of technology development to emerge during the years we've been researching and writing *Going Visual* is anytime, anywhere wireless connectivity.

THE CAMERA-PHONE PHENOMENON

We asked one of the most respected experts in the field, Tony Henning, managing editor of the *Future Image Mobile Imaging Report,* how the evolution of imaging devices from wired to wireless would affect the kind of typical business stories that we've described in *Going Visual.* He answered, "I think it's going to affect every single one by making the communication connection easier, faster, and more efficient."

He continued, "The camera phones entering the market today, with one- or two-megapixel resolution, can deliver a picture that is sufficient for uses like proving that your billboard is up or that your construction job is completed. This makes going around with a film camera and then taking the film in to be developed and then driving the prints somewhere and clipping them to a file totally obsolete. Now you can photograph it digitally and send the picture from the phone to an Internet site, coded in such a way that it immediately goes to a web page, which makes it available to everyone in the Community of Interest. Once the information is digital, you can publish it for the world. Wireless technology will also eliminate the need for digital camera users to drive back to the office, plug the card into a reader, and input the information into the system. Wireless allows you to save time and make the process more productive. Every human step is a place for somebody to make a mistake, 'Oh, I transposed the numbers and it didn't get attached to the Johnson account, it got attached to the Smith account.' If you do it from the phone, and that information is all programmed in with some kind of template, you make things more efficient, faster, and less prone to error."

Henning described how quickly camera phones, which are at the vanguard of the wireless imaging industry, have emerged as a worldwide phenomenon, and how fundamentally they are changing the dynamics of imaging, "A small Japanese phone company, J-Phone, started the ball rolling in 2000 by introducing the first camera phone, which consisted of a series of add-ons and gadgets that the Japanese market is so fond of. They started by plugging a little camera into a phone, and then they decided they could integrate the camera inside the phone. It was adopted much more rapidly than they imagined, catching the Japanese market by surprise; they were really unprepared for it. They didn't have a branding or marketing campaign to introduce it. In six months, before they had even decided to market it, a million people had bought camera phones.

"Every quarter, J-Phone would release sales figures that showed staggering growth: 4 million, then 7 million, then 9 million, and 12 million. It put them on the map, and it got the attention of the other Japanese carriers, KDDI and NTT DoCoMo; who started offering camera phones as well. As a result, Japanese subscribers responded in droves, and today close to 95 percent of all cell phones sold in Japan have cameras in them. It is difficult to find a cell phone without a camera in Japan. I have asked all three carriers, and all three do offer one or two models, mostly for prepaid customers, that don't have cameras in them, but it's virtually unheard of. If you go to any of those web sites and look at their phones, you have to dig pretty hard to find one without a camera. So, it became an absolute phenomenon in Japan. But even as this phenomenon was becoming known to markets outside of Japan, it was largely dismissed as another Japanese gadget fad. People in other parts of the world were asking, 'Why in the world would you want a camera in a phone?'

"The answer is that the camera phone has all kinds of implications for communications, for digital imaging, for social intercourse, for business. And, sure enough, from a phenomenon confined almost entirely to Japan, it has now become absolutely worldwide. All of the major carriers in the United States and Europe support camera phones, and manufacturers are producing hundreds of different models ranging from simple VGA (640 × 480 pixels) resolution phones to smart phones with video capture and 5-megapixel (2560 × 1920 pixels) resolution and dazzling 16-million color QVGA (240 × 320 pixel) screens. Even people in so-called emerging markets like India, China, Brazil, and Russia are adopting camera phones, and they're spending huge amounts of money, half their monthly salary in some cases, to get one. In these countries, users often leapfrog the terrible, ancient, wired telecommunications infrastructure, where it could take several years and cost thousands of dollars to get a wired phone. Now they just go out and get a prepaid phone with a phone card for virtually nothing and they are connected. Camera phones are becoming common enough and inexpensive enough that they can leapfrog directly to them."

Henning continued, "Because we carry our cell phones with us wherever we go . . . you have a camera with you whenever a picture-taking moment comes up. The thought 'I wish I had my camera' becomes the action, 'Look what I saw.' Because tens of millions of people now have cameras with them virtually all the time, there is an explosion in the number of pictures taken. We expect that over 70 billion images will be taken using camera phones in 2005. Early studies indicate that camera-phone users take more than twice as many pictures as digital or analog [film] camera users, and completely new uses are emerging, too. For example, here is an interesting way in which women use camera phones in Russia: When they are in a store buying new clothes, they want to make really sure that they're making the right purchase, because they don't have the kinds of return privileges that we have in the United States. So they go into the dressing rooms, try something on, take a picture with their camera phone, send it to the camera phones of their friends, their mother, their whole peer review group, and get back opinions in real time, before they actually make the purchase.

"The impact of camera phones on digital imaging in general is profound. In 2005 there will be roughly 375 million digital cameras sold worldwide; more than three quarters of them will be embedded in mobile phones. Sales of camera phones have more than doubled every year since their introduction in Japan in November 2000. From fewer than a million in 2000, there were over 180 million sold in 2004, and we project that at least 300 million will be sold in 2005— and 450 million in 2007. By 2006, we project that there will be 60 million camera phones in the United States. Going from essentially a gadget fad confined entirely to Japan in 2001 to the most popular picture-taking device around the world in five years is an unprecedented technology adoption record," Henning concluded.

Insights from the Mobile Imaging Summit

In November of 2004, *Future Image* held the most recent in its series of Mobile Imaging Summit conferences, which gather senior executives from the imaging, telecommunication, and computer

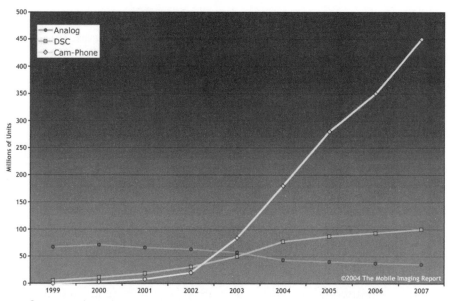

Camera sales: 1999–2007. *Source: Future Image Mobile Imaging Report*

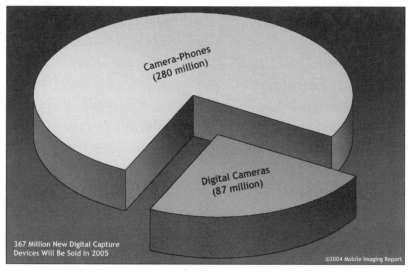

Capture device pie: 2005. *Source: Future Image Mobile Imaging Report*

industries together to brainstorm about the future of mobile imaging—the best possible place to gather insights into the latest thinking on the topic by industry insiders.

"This is potentially the biggest revolution since George Eastman started to think about imaging," according to T. Andrew Wilson, Kodak's director of worldwide strategy and business development. "This is such a unique point in time . . . it's not about the device anymore. When the application was only voice, it was about the device and the infrastructure. Now it's about the ecosystem far beyond those. The mobile imaging environment is the embodiment of the 'my pictures anytime, anywhere' vision. It's not about technology anymore, it's about how we define the system to be useful to people. These are the personal devices of multiple people within a household, or within an enterprise, who are always connected to the people and information that is important to them. If we can make the camera phone a primary camera, an imaging system, think in terms of people creating a trillion images a year. Roughly, there are 2 billion imaging devices out there right now creating something a little over 100 billion images. We know that in a few years there will be an installed base of a billion very capable camera phones, which should easily get us into an order of magnitude of a trillion images."

The reality of planning for and building an infrastructure to handle this explosion in image creation prompted IBM's global vice president of digital media, Gail Whipple, to identify a major area of focus going forward, "A trillion images represents a real challenge. What are you going to upload them to? Where are you going to store them? How are you going to wrap metadata or other indexing around them so that you can retrieve them later? How are you going to sort them and subcategorize them? We are going to require interoperability and a set of standards so that you can go from any device to any device, regardless of form factor, whether it is wireless or wired, whether it's a computer or a PDA or a camera phone, wherever you have a set of images that are going to travel over some transport, across a network. All these different devices have different form factors, and they all have different requirements in terms of being able to share."

Pierre Barbeau, general manager of Sprint's Picture Mail service, expanded on the notion of the ecosystem and the camera phone as a primary camera: "The planned migration for the camera phone in the next year or two is a change in behavior and expectation on the part of the consumer, such that they will take a camera phone with them when they plan to take pictures, whereas today they would grab a more traditional camera. The opportunity is to create an ecosystem around the device that will satisfy consumers regardless of whether they are at home, near a PC, or on the road traveling, and really give them the flexibility to choose how they want to use the device."

Barbeau then added some other elements to the mobile imaging mix, "We have introduced handsets that are capable of playing broadcast-like video and other TV-like functions to the handset. As network speeds increase, processing on the handsets improves, and displays get better, you can expect more of that broadcast-like video display functionality on the handset."

Adobe's senior vice president of digital imaging and video, Bryan Lamkin, was excited by the capabilities of camera phones to capture a video snapshot, "I think these phones are actually a big breakthrough in video, I think they are going to make video truly useful. Video is really not about sitting down and watching two hours of footage, it is really about finding the really meaningful 30 seconds and organizing that. I think the phones are a breakthrough in that area."

For every new opportunity and feature, there is a challenge. Gail Whipple pointed out, "Some of that content is going to be personal, person-to-person kind of content, but much of it is going to revolve around what new services are going to be offered—video clips, airline information, all kinds of things. When you start to think about downloading high-quality images you have to be concerned with digital rights management, business rights management, and the bandwidth to effectively enable all of that rich content to move around."

As amazing as these camera-phone devices are today, it's important to keep in perspective that from the standpoint of their product life cycle, they are still in their infancy. Drawing an analogy with personal computers, the current generation of products would be about where PCs were in 1985. There will be tremendous evolution over the next few years, shaped by what the technology is going to make possible and by what patterns emerge in terms of which functions users actually value. Imaging, text messaging, creating and interacting with documents, web access, and video creation and viewing are just some of the possibilities we've been presented with so far, but there are many more just over the horizon.

Attendees at the Mobile Imaging Summit were asked to evaluate five distinct and complementary evolutionary paths for the imaging functionality of wireless phones and other personal data devices. In each case, they were asked to conjecture whether that functionality is essentially here today or whether it will be delivered in one year, three years, or never—for either technical reasons or customer acceptance reasons.

FIVE EVOLUTIONARY CAMERA-PHONE PATHS

1. The ubiquitous camera

2. The wireless camera

3. The media phone

4. The visual analyzer

5. The visual phone

The first evolutionary path was defined as the *ubiquitous camera,* focusing on the fact that when a camera is embedded in the user's cell phone, he or she is likely to carry it at all times, unlike a traditional camera (film or digital), which is taken off the shelf only in preparation for a picture-taking occasion—be it a child's birthday, travel, or a special event. Having evaluated the performance of the many 1-megapixel camera phones provided for their use at the event by Nokia, and considering the recent introduction in Asia of 3- and 5-megapixel units, the majority of summit attendees (65 percent) declared the ubiquitous camera to be real today, an opinion shared broadly across all three industries represented. However, considering the weaknesses of today's camera phones compared to "pure" cameras, including the absence of lens cover, limitations of optical zoom lenses and flash components, and the difficulty in many cases of transferring images to a personal computer, significant minorities—16 and 19 percent, respectively— opted for the more conservative one-year and three-year time frames.

Overall sentiment was somewhat less bullish with respect to the *wireless Camera,* a consideration that focuses on the capability to offload images wirelessly, while shooting, directly from the capture device to a storage location or to a recipient, thus effectively eliminating (or at least reducing) the need for media, whether film or storage cards. While only a very small minority (2 percent) deemed this unlikely to ever materialize, most attendees somewhat cautiously forecast the emergence of this capability in either one year (33 percent) or three years (39 percent) down the road. However a significant minority of 26 percent declared it "here today," reflecting a difference of perception between the telecom attendees, among which 56 percent of respondents expressed that opinion, and the photo-imaging attendees, 75 percent of whom were in the one- and three-year camps.

The third category was defined as the *media phone,* highlighting these devices' ability to receive and display high-quality visual media, both still and video, ranging from news to sports clips to maps and directions and much more. Here, too, respondents from the telecommunications industry were most bullish, with the majority declaring the capability "here today," whereas photo-imaging respondents were evenly split between today, one-year, and three-year time frames. Computer industry respondents were primarily in the one-year and three-year camps. Overall, 37 percent of attendees voted for "here today," 33 percent voted for "one year," and 30 percent voted for "three years."

The majority of attendees (65 percent), spread fairly evenly across all three industry sectors, were clearly in the three-year camp with respect to the "visual analyzer," which focuses on the camera phone's ability to take a picture and to subsequently interpret patterns within the image—either in the device itself or through a remote server—and enable specific actions as a result. Examples include taking a picture of a bar code on a product and initiating a payment to purchase it, or reading an iris or thumbprint and passing it on to request a security clearance. Larry Lesley, senior vice president of consumer imaging and printing at Hewlett-Packard, offered this tantalizing concept, "One next step is text recognition. This means if I'm traveling in a foreign country I can point my camera phone at a sign that is in a foreign language, take a picture, and the camera phone will automatically translate the text for me." This kind of application takes the value of images as information to another level; 25 percent of respondents believe one year will be sufficient to attain this level of performance, while only 7 percent believe that it is here today, and only 3 percent believe that it will never happen.

Finally the most varied range of opinions was expressed with respect to the *visual phone,* a device that allows equal, easy, and instantaneous use of voice and images in a conversation—whether videoconference or real-time transmission of images or both—such that language and visuals combine to deliver the most effective person-to-person communication. The majority, 56 percent, believe this capability will be available within three years, and significant minorities of 13 percent and 17 percent, respectively, believe it is here today or will be within a year; another significant minority of

14 percent believe the visual phone to be unrealistic, the only evolutionary path to rate that degree of skepticism.

WIRELESS STANDARDS EXPLAINED

The camera phone is obviously the device that's captured global attention—it's the market that has all the scale, growing by leaps and bounds. But clearly, the concept of mobile imaging or visual communication without wires is not limited to the camera phone. A massive amount of development is going into wireless networks using technology such as WiFi and Bluetooth. All kind of devices, from digital cameras and printers to PCs and projectors, are going wireless. With the latest generation of WiFi- or Bluetooth-enabled data projectors, you can run a PowerPoint presentation from your phone, beam it to the projector, and have it on the screen for everybody in the meeting to see. Office buildings, coffee shops, hotels, airports, fast-food restaurants, and even entire cities are installing wireless networks so that, wherever you go, you're essentially connected.

Wireless connectivity is appearing seemingly everywhere these days. The goal is to connect everything—MP3 player, car, TV, wallet, navigational system, printer, corner kiosk, universal remote control, camcorder, stereo, checkout counter, DVR, car audio system, portable video player, headset, garage door opener, digital camera, cell phone, PDA, laptop, and of course your PC—at home, at the office, and on the move. The promise of wireless is to eliminate the wires and let all our electronic gadgets talk to each other and exchange information and content automatically and seamlessly. Because there are so many wireless technology terms bandied about in the press these days (e.g., Bluetooth, WiFi, GSM, ZigBee, WiMAX, UWB, CDMA, infrared, and 3G), we thought it would be helpful to provide a basic glossary of terms, and we asked Tony Henning to decode the alphabet soup of wireless standards.

Wireless transmitters and receivers all communicate by using signals that travel over different slices of the electromagnetic spectrum, different radio frequencies, like the stations on your radio dial. The following technologies are categorized by how far the signals can—or are intended to—travel.

Wireless Personal Area Network (WPAN)

A WPAN operates in a bubble that extends up to 10 meters (about 33 feet) from the device. The radios that serve this personal space are generally low power and low cost. The wired equivalent is a short cable, like the one that connects your headphones to your stereo, for instance.

- Bluetooth is the one most often bandied about these days. Bluetooth was developed by phone companies to let your earphone connect to your cell phone without plugging it in. The initial specifications were developed by Scandinavian telecom firms, which may help to explain the odd name. Bluetooth gets its catchy name from Harald Blåtand (Bluetooth), the first Christian Danish king who united Denmark and Norway in the tenth century. The name was chosen because Bluetooth is supposed to unite the worlds of computing and telecommunications, just as old Harald Bluetooth united Denmark and Norway. After years of hype, the technology is finally starting to achieve significant market penetration—more than 2 million Bluetooth-equipped devices now ship every week. The primary weakness of the technology for visual communications is that it is relatively slow, capable of transferring just 90 kilobytes of data per second. Using Bluetooth (at its maximum theoretical data rate), it would take about 3.5 seconds to transfer a highly compressed 1-megapixel (1,024 × 1,024 pixels) image.

  Network speeds—also called *data rates, bandwidth,* or *throughput*—are almost always expressed as the amount of information that can be transferred per unit of time, generally in kilobits or megabits (not bytes) per second. We translate the rates into kilobytes per second, as file sizes are generally expressed in bytes, not bits. The rates given are usually the maximum theoretical rate, not the actual, real-world rate that you get when you use the network. Networks that are fast are sometimes called *broadband* because they have lots of bandwidth: They are fat pipes capable of carrying lots of information in a short span of time. Networks that are slow have low, or narrow, bandwidth, thin pipes that can carry relatively little information. Think fire hose versus drinking straw.

- Bluetooth gets all the press coverage, but infrared is the most common technology in this space, communicating between your remote control and your TV or stereo, your car key and the door lock, or from PDA to PDA. Infrared is in virtually every cell phone in Japan, so the Japanese can use their *keitai* (mobile phones) to control their TVs and DVRs. Infrared devices must be within a few feet of each other and have a clear line of sight. Data rates vary substantially, from a fraction of a kilobyte (0.002) to 0.5 megabyte per second. Given such a wide range of speeds, transferring a highly compressed megapixel image could take anywhere from a day and a half to less than a second. Despite being deployed in tens of millions of devices for more than a decade, infrared is seriously underutilized.

- UWB (ultra wideband) is a short-range radio technology that sends extremely short bursts of data at low power over a very wide swath of spectrum. UWB's combination of broader spectrum and lower power improves speed and reduces interference with other wireless technologies. Ultrawideband radio not only can carry a huge amount of data at very low power, but also has the ability to carry signals through doors, walls, and other obstacles that tend to reflect other radio signals. In the United States, the Federal Communications Commission (FCC) has mandated that UWB radio transmissions can legally operate in the range from 3.1 GHz up to 10.6 GHz, at a limited transmit power of −41dBm/MHz. Because of its very high data rates—currently around 500Mbps (62.5MB per second)—UWB is seen as ideal for transferring multimedia content around a wireless home entertainment network. Using UWB at current rates, it would take about 0.005 seconds to transfer one highly compressed megapixel (1,024 × 1,024 pixels) image.

As is relatively common in the early commercialization of any technology—think Betamax versus VHS—interested companies have coalesced around two competing specifications for the IEEE 802.15.3a standard. The MBOA (MultiBand OFDM Alliance) has formed a special interest group (SIG) with 170 members, including heavyweights like Hewlett-Packard, Intel, Nokia, Philips, Samsung, Sony, and Texas Instruments, and has the backing of industry groups like the WiMedia Alliance, Wireless USB Promoter Group, and 1394 Trade Association. The rival technology is backed by Freescale Semiconductor, Motorola's former Semiconductor Products Sector, which has taken its version to market with a number of manufacturing partners in Taiwan.

Wireless Local Area Network (WLAN)

A WLAN operates over distances of up to 100 meters (roughly 328 feet). The radios in this area are generally much faster and more powerful than those in the WPAN category. The wired equivalent is the Ethernet cabling that supports your office or home network.

- WiFi is the dominant technology in this space, all but eliminating competing technologies like Home RF and Hyperlan. WiFi is the marketing term for the 802.11 family of wireless Ethernet standards specified by the Institute of Electrical and Electronic Engineers (IEEE). It stands for *wireless fidelity*—an effort to make the technology sound as familiar as HiFi, or *high fidelity*. Although there have been some notable failures among firms hoping to cash in on its growing popularity, WiFi is nonetheless becoming ubiquitous. It is the technology behind the tens of thousands of "hot spots" at Starbucks, Borders, McDonald's, airport lounges, and hotels around the world. Whole campuses, neighborhoods, communities, and even an island nation (Niue, for five months) have gone WiFi. WiFi networks are better suited to transferring visual information because they're much faster than WPANs, transferring from 1.4 to 6.8 megabytes of data per second, and even faster versions are on their way. Using WiFi, you can transfer anywhere from four to more than twenty-two 1-megapixel images a second. The primary challenge for WiFi to overcome is security concerns. Too many people and companies don't take proper measures to prevent unauthorized users from breaking into the network and stealing either bandwidth or sensitive information.

- ZigBee is starting to get some attention, mostly because of the catchy name. (The ZigBee Principle is the technique—a zigzag dance—used by honeybees to communicate a newfound food source to other bees in the hive.) This technology is designed to be an ultracheap, ultra-low-power, very simple method for monitoring and control devices to communicate, machine-to-machine—TV remote controls, wireless keyboards, lighting controls, patient monitors, and the like. It has no real application to visual communications because it is ultraslow. Depending on the frequency, ZigBee transfers between 5 and 30 kilobytes per second. Using ZigBee, it would take anywhere from 10 seconds to more than a minute to transfer that 1-megapixel image.

Wireless Wide Area Network (WWAN)

A WWAN operates over distances measured in miles, not meters. The primary technology in this space, of course, is the cellular telephone network that covers most population centers and highways. Most major urban markets are served by as many as six or more such networks. These networks are called *cellular* because the coverage area is divided into a grid of cells, like graph paper, each with its own base station and tower or antenna. Each telephone in the cell communicates with the base station. If the phone moves to another cell, the call is automatically transferred to the base station in the new cell. This system was first proposed by Bell Labs as early as 1947 to allow wireless operators to reuse their very limited frequency bands. The process by which the Mobile Telephone Switching Office (MTSO) passes a cellular phone connection from one radio frequency in one cell to another radio frequency in another is called a *handoff*. If your call is dropped, it's generally during the handoff. Two technologies account for the majority of cellular networks worldwide.

1. Global system for mobile communications (GSM), originally developed as a pan-European standard for digital mobile telephony, has become the world's most widely used mobile system and the de facto standard in Europe and Asia. GSM was first introduced in 1991 and is now used by 72 percent of the world's wireless market—more than 1.2 billion subscribers in 205 countries and territories. In the United States, Cingular, AT&T (soon to be part of Cingular), and T-Mobile use GSM technology and its follow-on technologies, GPRS, EDGE, and UMTS. Together the three carriers have around 63 million subscribers.

2. Code division multiple access (CDMA) is a wideband spread-spectrum technology that allows multiple users across the broadcast spectrum by assigning each a unique code. Theoretically, CDMA has three times more capacity than GSM, and 9 to 15 times that of analog. CDMA is a military technology first used during World War II by the English to foil German attempts at

jamming transmissions. The Allies decided to transmit over several frequencies instead of one, making it difficult for the Germans to pick up the complete signal. Because Qualcomm Inc. created communications chips for CDMA technology, it was privy to the classified information. Once the information became public, Qualcomm claimed patents on the technology and became the first to commercialize it. CDMA is used by about 220 million subscribers, primarily in Asia and North America. In the United States, Sprint and Verizon use CDMA technologies and have more than 65 million subscribers between them.

The historical progression of cellular networks, both GSM and CDMA, are as follows:

- First-generation (1G) refers to the original analog, circuit-switched mobile phone networks such as TACS (United Kingdom), NMT (Scandinavia), and AMPS (United States). Voice links were poor, handoff unreliable, capacity low, and security nonexistent.

- Second-generation (2G) refers to the digital mobile phone networks such as GSM, PDC (Japan), and CDMA. 2G networks support high bit rate voice and limited data communications. They offer auxiliary services such as data, fax, SMS, and MMS. Most 2G protocols offer different levels of encryption.

- Sometimes used to refer to networks between 2G and 3G, 2.5G protocols extend 2G systems to provide additional features such as packet-switched connections and enhanced data rates. GPRS and EDGE, for example, are 2.5G technologies between GSM and W-CDMA.

- Third-generation (3G) is supposed to refer to cellular networks that meet the minimum performance capabilities defined by the International Telecommunications Union

(ITU), an agency of the United Nations that deals with regulatory matters, standardization, and spectrum allocations on a global scale. IMT-2000, as the specification is known, mandates data speeds of 144 kbps at driving speeds, 384 kbps for outside stationary use or walking speeds, and 2 Mbps indoors. Those speeds are designed to allow for advanced services like video telephony and streaming multimedia. Many cellular carriers, however, are simply defining 3G by significant jumps in access rates, so 3G is loosely applied to all wideband mobile telecommunication services that are even slightly faster than 2G. The initial goal for 3G, for the greater good of global communications and interoperability, was for all the telecommunications manufacturers and providers (and all governments and international standards bodies) to agree on one next-generation standard—a converged 3G. That goal has proven elusive. Although five 3G specifications have been approved, the most likely outcome is a tri-mode system, dictating a migration path dependent on your legacy system. GSM networks will migrate to UMTS (W-CDMA); CDMA networks will migrate to CDMA 1x EV-DO or EV-DV; and at least some Chinese networks will likely migrate to TD-SCDMA.

• WiMAX is a standards-based wireless technology that provides high-throughput broadband connections over long distances. WiMAX can be used for a number of applications, including last-mile broadband connections, hotspot and cellular backhaul, and high-speed enterprise connectivity for businesses. An implementation of the IEEE 802.16 standard, WiMAX provides metropolitan area network connectivity at speeds of up to 75 Mb/sec. WiMAX systems can be used to transmit signal as far as 30 miles. However, on average, a WiMAX base-station installation will likely cover between three and five miles.

Index

About the Authors

Alexis Gerard occupies a unique place in the modern history of imaging. For the past 14 years, his visionary thinking about the convergence of photography and information technology has had a major influence on business leaders both inside and outside the imaging industry.

A passionate photographer since his twenties, Gerard founded his imaging think tank, Future Image Inc., in 1991, after holding executive positions in new technologies marketing with Apple Computer during the company's heyday of innovation, which included the development of the Macintosh. Today, Future Image is the acknowledged leading independent center of expertise on the convergence of imaging, technology, and business. Executives, entrepreneurs, and investors worldwide rely for their decision making on its continuous information services (the Future Image Executive Information Service and the Future Image Wireless Imaging Research Edition), its research studies, and the advice of its consultants. The company is the official information and research partner of the International Imaging Industry Association (I3A).

Gerard is also widely known in business circles as the leading independent authority on the future of imaging. His opinions have been quoted at various times in the *Wall Street Journal, New York Times, Boston Globe, San Francisco Chronicle, International Herald Tribune, USA Today, Financial Times, Newsweek, Business Week,* and many other publications.

Gerard's public speaking engagements have included executive gatherings of associations such as the Society for Information Science and Technology and corporations such as Agfa, Apple, Conexant, Hewlett-Packard,

Intel, Minolta, Polaroid, Procter and Gamble, and others worldwide. He chaired the inaugural conference of the Digital Imaging Marketing Association in 1995, and delivered one of two keynotes (the other being Nicholas Negroponte of the MIT Media Lab). In 2002 he chaired the Future Image/Forbes Visual Communication Executive Summit, and participated in the opening panel of Photokina alongside the CEOs of Kodak, Fuji, Epson, Agfa, and IBM's Digital Media Division.

Most recently he launched the Mobile Imaging Executive Summit, a by-invitation executive conference held three times yearly (Americas, Europe, Asia), which has the unique distinction of gathering senior executives from the imaging, information processing, telecommunications, and entertainment industries.

Gerard is a member of the International Advisory Council of the George Eastman House. From 1997 to 1998, he held the positions of President and Executive Director of the Digital Imaging Group (DIG), an open nonprofit industry consortium founded by Adobe, Canon, Eastman Kodak, Fuji, Hewlett-Packard, IBM, Intel, Live Picture, and Microsoft to promote the growth of digital imaging into mainstream markets. The DIG is now merged into the I3A (International Imaging Industry Association).

Bob Goldstein is well known in the digital imaging industry as both an executive and a featured speaker on the subject of Visual Communication. He was president and founder of ZZYZX Visual Systems in Los Angeles, California, where he pioneered businesses in high-volume image scanning, digital retouching, stock photo databases and digital distribution networks, fine art digital printing, interactive media projects, web site design, and digital photo studios. He then became president of the Altamira Group, which produced the Genuine Fractals line of digital image scaling and compression software. In these executive positions he worked closely with industry leaders to help determine the future of imaging.

Through his public speaking engagements and one-on-one sessions he has inspired thousands of photographers and hundreds of businesses to "go digital" and make the transition from traditional, film-based photography to digital imaging. He has given lectures and workshops on the subjects covered in *Going Visual* across the United States and Canada, appearing in

Photo by Ira Nowinski

Bob Goldstein and Alexis Gerard

cities such as New York, San Francisco, Atlanta, Dallas, Boston, Houston, Washington, DC, Las Vegas, San Diego, Seattle, Portland, Philadelphia, Orlando, Chicago, Pittsburgh, Los Angeles, Toronto, Montreal, and Vancouver. His corporate clients include Eastman Kodak, Apple Computer, Oracle Corp, Microsoft, and Hewlett-Packard. He is a senior analyst for *The Future Image Report,* for whom he authored an industry study of Internet visual search engines. He has appeared at many conferences, including Seybold, PMA, DIMA, MacWorld, Siggraph, PhotoEast, and the Lyra Summit, and has also appeared on CNNfn. Goldstein has a business degree from the University of Southern California.